Beach Blanket Atheism

The Beginner's Guide for the Non-Believer

by
Edward P. Tolley, Jr.

Cartoons by Jeff Swenson

CYNTOMEDIA CORPORATION

Pittsburgh, PA

ISBN 1-58501-043-X

Trade Paperback
© Copyright 2003 Edward P. Tolley, Jr.
All Rights Reserved
First Printing — 2003
Library of Congress #20021134638

Request for information should be addressed to:

SterlingHouse Publisher, Inc.
7436 Washington Avenue
Pittsburgh, PA 15218
www.sterlinghousepublisher.com

CeShore is an imprint of SterlingHouse Publisher, Inc.

SterlingHouse Publisher, Inc. is a company
of the CyntoMedia Corporation.

Book Design: Kathleen M. Gall
Cover Design: Eric C. Moresea—SterlingHouse Publisher, Inc.

Printed in the United States of America

BEACH BLANKET ATHEISM

A Pocket Guide to Free-Thinking

Everything You've Always Wanted to Know about Atheism but were Afraid to Ask

Nothing else to buy! Nothing to join!

If you can read this sentence, you can understand it.

Gain an extra few hours every week!

Lose five pounds of guilt in a single hour!

*Guaranteed to make you think,
whether you're good at it or not.*

Easy to read—no long sentences, no small print.

Cartoons by Jeff Swenson

"I'm going to send a copy to each of my wife's relatives."
Douglas Tolley, Buena Vista, OK

"What a fool I've been all these years! Thank you so much!"
Kenneth Tolley, Greenville, NC

"Pure, unadulterated barf!"
Lee Tolley, Aurora, CO

"Who's going to buy this book—have you thought of that?"
Nancy Jobstle Tolley, Port Washington, NY

*"I'm going to send a copy to my fiancée, who's been trying
to pick a church for two years now."*
Henry ("Knuckles") Tolley, Peoria, IL

*"If you think atheism is fun,
you may be ready for sky-diving!"*
Hank Tolley, Brooklyn, NY

"My kids turned out rotten after 15 years of Sunday School."
Mortimer Tolley, Conshohocken, PA

*"You're welcome to my editorial comments,
but just don't put my name in it, okay?"*
(name withheld)

*"What a load off my mind!
It's like I can think without even trying!"*
Agnes Tolley, Dover, DE

"Well, I wouldn't have written it exactly like you did."
Prof. Archibald G. F. Tolley, Cambridge, MA

*"You were a smart-ass when you worked for me, but I never
thought you would stoop to this unGodly trash!"*
Erickson Contractors, Geneva, IL

"I am praying for you ten times a day."
Sister Agatha (name of church withheld)

*"I bought 50 of your blasphemous books and burned every
one of them!"*
Timothy D. O'Rourke, Boston, MA

CONTENTS

I owe this book to a fortuitous encounter with Shirley, the proprietor of my local airport newsstand. After two full years without a vacation, I was at last waiting for a plane bound for San Francisco and, ultimately, Tahiti, where I would cleanse my brain of bullshit overload. After checking out all the paperback books available and finding nothing to pique my interest—and, of course, ascertaining that there was nothing uplifting or healthy to do—I patronized the bar. The man next to me, who just missed the start of his round-the-world business trip, said to me, glassy-eyed, grasping a thick bundle of tickets: "There is no God!" I had the funny feeling he was on to something.

"There's nothing good to read in this airport," I said to Shirley afterward. "I'm just starting my vacation and I need a light, funny book."

"There's lots of nice books and 'zines in my news boutique," she informed me, "which I just closed. Everything a normal person would want."

"Can you re-open it?" I asked.

"What tickles your fancy, mister? There's model magazines under the counter, special-interest stuff, either brand new or like new. I got plain brown wrappers, too. But I ain't re-opening for just one little-bitty girly mag, if you know what I mean."

"I need something to read on the beach, something as far away from my daily existence as possible. Like, how about a good simple book about the Big Bang, or how the pyramids were built, or say, atheism? Like, you know, is it just another religion, or what? I mean, can the pointy-headed scientists and professors be as crazy as Pat Robertson and Jerry Falwell?"

"There's no such book, and I know my business. If you want trash like that, go write it yourself!"

So I did! Down there on the beach, under the palm trees, it was easy to outline. Why shouldn't atheism be as funny as religion, or other self-help books? How could atheism be worse, in fact, than a book that tells you how to re-wire your soul, which scientists tell us does not exist? The idea is really very simple: what do the smartest people in the world really think? In fact, few people know what the smartest people in the world think because they write books only for each other! (That is why ordinary people have to read books by hustlers like Deepak Chopra).

As I sat there on the gorgeous beach taking in the timeless ocean, the Ultimate Truth occurred to me: what you see is what you get! By the time my vacation was over, the overall plan of the book was complete, so all I had to do was look up jokes and quotations by famous people at my public library and on the Internet. Now you can take this book with you to the beach on your vacation. Stare at the horizon at sunset and realize for the first time that the world is real, and consists only of real things, like the scientists tell us. It will not go away if you stop praying. Remember: beach blanket atheism is to god what beach blanket bingo is to chastity!

Ludwig Wittgenstein, I discovered, said that a book on philosophy could be entirely composed of jokes, which is a good example of something theoretical and impractical, like philosophy. While I did not originally intend to put Wittgenstein's theory into practice here, I admit that his statement—like Shirley's—inspired and challenged me. What I found was that the jokes or funny bits have to be connected somehow by ordinary sentences. (Of course, Wittgenstein did not say how many pages his book would be; the "book" he had in mind might have been a ten-page pamphlet for all I know, which any fool could write.)

However, this is not intended to be a neutral discussion of the question whether god exists; it reflects the majority view of scientists and university scholars that god does not exist. As everybody knows by know, there are no serious debates about the existence of god in our great universities' science departments. If that is news to you, read this book! It would be pointless for me to question the conclusions reached by the most eminent thinkers of our time, including, for example, Einstein, Bertrand Russell, Antony Flew, Steven Pinker, Stephen Jay Gould, Allen Bloom, and Prof. Paul Kurtz, to name just a few. *In order to avoid mistakes, I have copied everything, and invented nothing.* All I have done is to add connecting thoughts, or bridges, to other people's ideas, including also the ideas of Woody Allen, Groucho Marx, Mark Twain and other level-headed people.

This book will be most useful for someone who never studied philosophy in college, or for someone who never went to college, or for an entering freshman, as well as for people on vacation at the beach. (Why not use your beach time to get a head start on life? Why assume that Jesus is watching over you, when it's really some Congressional committee, the IRS or the Department of Homeland Security?) I am willing to bet my next paycheck that there are no other books out there like this. Big words like "epistemology" are not in this book. *

On the other hand, if you're the kind of person who thinks UFO's, astrology, talking to your dead uncle, etc., are "real," you are not intelligent enough to read even this simple book. (I'm surprised you got this far!) If you happen to be in college and think those things are real, consider dropping out.

Finally, a note of thanks to Rev. Timothy O'Rourke, for his advance purchase of 50 books, sight unseen, which I took to the bank.

---

*I don't mean for you to look for it and win real money. I have proofread it five times and "epistemology" is not in it. I am only trying to make the point that big words like that are not in this neat, simple vacation-time book.

CHAPTER 1

AGNOSTICISM

> "As men's prayers are a disease of the will, so
> are their creeds a disease of the intellect ...
> Whoso would be a man must be a noncon-
> formist."
>
> **—Ralph Waldo Emerson**

You will never find an agnostic on your doorstep, like a Jehovah's Witness, because agnosticism is not a religion or an organization. If you could cross a Jehovah's witness with an agnostic, what would you get? *Someone who rings* your *doorbell for no reason*, meaning that agnostics have no religious beliefs and don't want to convert you. (What do you get when you cross an insomniac, an agnostic, and a dyslexic? Answer: Someone who lies awake all night wondering if there *really* is a *Dog*.)

Agnostics are defined by what they do *not know*, rather than what they do know. Agnostics say "I don't know if there is a god" because they are honest. Mort Sahl said, "Most people past college age are not atheists because, for one thing, you don't get any days off. And if you're an agnostic, you don't *know* whether you get them off or not." We are all agnostics about things we don't *know*, like how the Big Bang occurred, or how Jesse Ventura got elected governor of Minnesota, or how computers work, etc.

"Have you ever heard a radio talk show host call himself an agnostic? Do you know what an agnostic is? In the radio talk show business an agnostic is someone who just got out of a meeting in the general manager's office," said Professor Leykis. People just don't like to be associated with ideas out of the mainstream, like the flat earth cult. It sounds better to say you're a skeptic. (College philosophy students ask: "How many skeptics does it take to change a light bulb?" The answer is: "Maybe none, if the bulb is just not screwed in well." (A lot of perfectly good light bulbs, like good ideas, are discarded because people are not logical.)

Joseph Lewis, a prominent 19th century atheist, said "Is it not better to place a question mark upon a problem while seeking an answer than to put the label "God" there and consider the matter closed?"

In recent times, agnosticism has become the rule, rather than the exception, for prominent thinkers, writers and commentators on the state of American reality. Jefferson said "Question with boldness even the existence of God; because if there be one, He must approve homage of Reason rather than that of blindfolded Fear." Sam Butler said "Prayers are to men as dolls are to children. They are not without use and comfort, but it is not easy to take them very seriously." Shaw said "The fact that a believer is happier than a skeptic is no more to the point than the fact that a drunken man is happier than a sober one."

Chaz Bufe defined an agnostic as "A person who feels superior to atheists by merit of his ignorance of the rules of logic and evidence." Charlie Chaplin said "By simple common sense I don't believe in God, in none." Butler also said "If God wants us to do a thing, He should make his wishes sufficiently clear. Sensible people will wait till He has done this before paying much attention to Him." Henry Ward Beecher said "There was never such a gigantic lie told as the fable of the Garden of Eden." Russell Baker said "In ruder days, disputes about what constituted a fully qualified Christian often led to sordid quarrels in which the disputants tortured, burned and hanged each other in the conviction that torture, burning and hanging were Christian things to do ..." To Dick Cavett, religion was like a fix—"Knowing it could instantly make me much happier makes it somehow unworthy of having."

Agnosticism Is A Matter Of "Knowing" Or "Not Knowing."

Agnosticism is not a mere matter of opinion, but a question of *knowledge*, which comes from the Latin word *gnoscere* and the Greek word *gnosis*. You cannot logically say, "although I have no knowledge of god, I believe in god." That is like saying, "I have no knowledge of how democracy works but I believe in democracy."

Thomas H. Huxley defined it as follows: "Agnosticism, in fact, is not a creed, but a method, the essence of which lies in the rigorous application of a single principle. That principle is of great antiquity; it is as old as Socrates, as old as the writer who said: Try all things, hold fast by that which is good; it is the foundation of the Reformation, which simply illustrated the axiom that every man should be able to give a reason for the faith that is in him; it is the great principle of Descartes; it is the fundamental axiom of modern science. Positively the principle may be expressed: In matters of the intellect, *follow your reason as far as it will take you*, without regard to any other consideration. And negatively: In matters of the intellect, do not pretend that conclusions are certain which are not demonstrated or demonstrable. When there is evidence, no one speaks of "faith" ... . We do not speak of faith that two and two are four or that the earth is round," he said.

Clarence Darrow, the eminent lawyer who defended Mr. Scopes in the 1929 evolution trial, said "I do not consider it an insult, but rather a compliment to be called an agnostic. I do not pretend to know what many ignorant men are sure of—that is all that agnosticism means." T. H. Huxley said "Agnosticism simply means that a man shall not say he knows or believes that for which he has no ground for professing to believe."

Agnosticism is only an admission that the human mind is not capable of knowing god. Humans know god only by way of hearsay, because there is no evidence of god. It is the first step in a quest to understand how the world works. *To prove you're not agnostic, all you have* to *do is obtain knowledge of god.*

When it comes to good reasoning about god, the best book I have found is *God: A Critical Inquiry,* by Antony Flew, who said "To say that someone knows something is to say no more than that he claims to know it or that he believes it most strongly. It is to say also both that it is true and that he is in a position to know that it is true. So neither the sincerity of his conviction nor the ingenuousness of his utterance guarantees that he really knew." Thus, when Billy Graham preaches that he knows there is a god, he is saying "nothing" *because he is not in a position* to *know if god exists any more than anybody else is.*

God Cannot Be Known By Humans

The human brain is not equipped to see invisible things, such as god. Thomas Aquinas himself acknowledged that the idea of god is not necessary to understand how the world works: "But it seems that everything we see in the world can be accounted for by other principles, supposing god did not exist. For all natural things can be reduced to one principle, which is nature, and all voluntary things can be reduced to one principle, which is human reason, or will. Therefore there is no need to suppose God's existence." Aquinas became religious because he *wanted* to become religious, which people still do today.

Some people go to church to meet pretty girls, or because their boss goes there, etc.

Bertrand Russell said "The atheist, like a Christian, holds that we can know whether or not there is a god. The Christian holds that we can know there is a god; the atheist, that we can know there is not. The agnostic suspends judgment, saying that there are not sufficient grounds either for affirmation or for denial ... an agnostic may hold that the existence of god, though not impossible, is very improbable; he may even hold it so improbable that it is not worth considering in practice." Russell also wrote: "Atheists are not agnostics ... The atheist holds that we know that god does not exist. *But the agnostic holds that we do not know enough either* to *affirm* or *deny the existence of a Supreme Being* ... I believe that although the existence of god is not impossible, it is improbable. Quite improbable."

George Smith wrote: "The theist is positing the *unknowable,* that which is beyond man's comprehension, that which man will never be able to understand regardless of his degree of knowledge. Since the supernatural must remain forever outside the context of man's knowledge, a "supernatural explanation" is a contradiction in terms. One cannot explain the unknown with reference to the unknowable." Flew said in his book *How to Think Straight:* "To explain the unknown by the known is a logical procedure; to explain the known by the unknown is a form of theological lunacy." Pascal said "If we submit everything to reason, our religion will have no mysterious and supernatural element."

The reason people differ about the nature of god is that, god being imaginary, each person imagines a slightly different one. A universal religion that makes sense to all people is not possible *because different people cannot be made* to *see imaginary things in exactly the same way.* If god gave us brains for thinking, why does thinking lead to agnosticism? Agnosticism always holds out the possibility that god might suddenly give us knowledge of his existence, as summed up by the following lyrics by E. Y. Harburg that were popular in the early 20th century: "No matter how I probe and probe / I cannot quite believe in god / But Oh! I hope to god that he / Unswervingly believes in me."

"To believe is very dull. To doubt is intensely engrossing," said Oscar Wilde. Agnostics are mentally healthy, not spooked by superstition, and can look at Bible stories objectively, like Jerry Seinfeld does: "God fixed up Adam with Eve. She's nice. She's very free about her body, doesn't wear much. She was going out with this real snake, but I think that's over." Many agnostics are just cautious doubters, like Woody Allen, who said "I don't believe in the afterlife, although I am bringing a change of underwear."

Shaw said "Heaven, as conventionally conceived, is a place so inane, so dull, so useless, so miserable, that nobody has ever ventured to describe a whole day in heaven, though plenty of people have described a day at the seaside." Sir Philip Sidney's version of heaven was eating foie gras to the sound of trumpets. The writer of a recent *New York Times Magazine* article on how people think of heaven, Camille Sweeney, said she could imagine seeing all the saints, including St. Peter. "Saw you by the pool this morning. You look fabulous." Andrew Greeley, the religious author, said "Heaven's going to look like a big city by a lake, something like Chicago, not at all like Manhattan." Frank McCourt said "My hereafter is here. I am where I'm going, for I am mulch. It's a great comfort to know that in my mulch-hood I may nourish a row of parsnips." Geraldo Rivera told that reporter: "I'm not sure what a Heaven would be like, but hell, hell might be interesting—a lot like the news business."

Religion Is Contrary To Human Nature And Natural Desire

If religion is good, why is living life without religion so much fun? Camus said "If there is a sin against life, it consists perhaps not so much in despairing of life as in hoping for another life and in eluding the implacable grandeur of this life." Madonna said "It is difficult to believe in a religion that places such a high premium on chastity and virginity." She also said "When I get down on my knees, it is not to pray." Billy Joel said "I'd rather laugh with the sinners than cry with the saints. The sinners are much more fun."

If god wants his message delivered to all humans, why does he pick spokesmen like Jerry Falwell, Pat Robertson and other uneducated buffoons as his spokesmen? Jimmy Buffet wrote "Religion, religion ... Oh, there's a fine line between Saturday night and Sunday morning ... Where's the church, who took the steeple? Religion's in the hands of some crazy-ass people, television preachers with bad hair and dimples. The God's honest truth is, it's not that simple." "If the lord had meant us to have faith, he'd have given us lobotomies," said Zlatko.

If god made us, why did he make us so bad? "We must question the logic of having an all-knowing, all-powerful God, who creates faulty humans, and then blames them for his own mistakes," said Gene Roddenberry. "If god made us to listen to him, why do children lack an antenna to catch god's vibes? It is an interesting and demonstrable fact that all children are atheists and were religion not inculcated into their minds, they would remain so," said Ernestyne Rose. "If there is a God, He is infinitely incomprehensible, having neither parts nor limits," wrote Pascal. Emanual Kant, a founder of contemporary philosophy, said (hundreds of years ago): "We can have no knowledge of something that can't be seen or heard or felt. Therefore, He has no relation to us. We are therefore incapable of knowing what He is, or whether He is ... We cannot *know* God, for knowledge is confined to the sensible, phenomenal world ..." Lincoln, one of America's intellectual and moral giants, said "It will not do to investigate the subject of religion too closely, as it is apt to lead to infidelity." The problem is that there is nothing to study or measure.

Knowledge Of The Bible Is Not Knowledge Of God

Seminarians do not "study" the question whether god exists. Religion *assumes* that god exists and then concerns itself with wondering what god is like and what he wants us to do. The Christian religion is not a philosophy of life based on rational thought, but an explanation of what god wants based on the assumption that the Bible represents "knowledge," like a railroad schedule, for example. *All religions differ because nobody really has knowledge.* The Christian religion is not a philosophy of life based on rational thought, but an explanation of what god wants based on the assumption that the Bible represents "knowledge" and "truth." That sounds simple, and everybody should agree with it. Those with knowledge of god, raise your right hands!

The actual, hard knowledge of religious leaders is limited to the conduct of prayer and other ceremonies, which is under their control. If the Bible is the word of god, then they have knowledge of god. But if the Bible is just another manmade book, they only have knowledge of another manmade book. Thus it is perfectly possible for an educated, sane person to read the Bible from cover to cover and conclude that he knows what's in the Bible but hasn't a clue about god.

Aristotle wrote: "All human actions have one or more of these seven causes: chance, nature, compulsion, habit, reason, passion, desire." Note that these do not include god unless you call him "chance."

Religious Devotion Does Not Lead To Knowledge Or "Meaning"

Most people seem to think that thinking about something for a long time will eventually produce knowledge about it. It is just the opposite," Carlyle said. "Just in the ratio knowledge increases, faith decreases." You can study religion all your life and never have a clue about how the world really works. *All you learn is how your religion works, not how the world works* or *how god works!* In India and Tibet millions of people devote their lives to preparing for an after-life, chanting and mumbling prayers, waiting for their real lives to begin the day they die! An old guy in a dirty *dhoti* can say, "Who are you to argue with me? I who have spent 40 years doing nothing but praying and contemplating the universe (mumbling 'oom ta, oom ga,' etc.)" Gullible people say "He must be right because I have spent only one hour contemplating the universe!"

Gibbon wrote: "The evidence of the heavenly witnesses—the Father, the Word, and the Holy Ghost—would now be rejected in any court of Justice." Edison, a very smart, practical kind of guy, wrote: My mind is incapable of conceiving such a thing as a soul. I may be in error, and man may have a soul; but I simply do not believe it ... I have never seen the slightest scientific proof of the religious theories of heaven and hell, of future life for individuals, or of a personal God ... Religion is all bunk." Many people, of course, like to have it both ways. Ernest Renan, for example, said "Lord, if there is a Lord, save my soul, if I have a soul." The question is, wrote Nietzsche: "Which is it: Is man one of God's blunders, or is God one of man's blunders?" Even in pre-Christian times, there was widespread skepticism about the gods. "It is ridiculous to suppose that the great head of things, whatever it be, pays any regard to human affairs," said Pliny the Elder. Christopher Marlowe wrote: "I count religion but a childish toy, and hold there is no sin but ignorance."

Christian Fundamentalist hellfire and religious devotion also may have the effect of numbing the mind, for a few hours at least, because of its effect on the senses. "The only force more devastating than a nuclear holocaust is a group of Christians fresh out of church," said Matt Polek. (At just that moment they may be incapable of rational thought because the sermon has replaced everything they ever learned about life. (Don't be caught just then drinking, smoking, kissing, fondling, swearing, picketing, singing, dancing, or playing cards!)

"I cannot be angry at God, in whom I do not believe," said Simone de Beauvoir. George Smith, in his book "Atheism—the Case Against God," put it this way: "The Christian faces this dilemma: if he wishes to retain the notion of a supernatural being, he must insist that God's nature is incomprehensible. On the other hand, if the Christian wishes to escape the plight of agnosticism (which he must to give meaning to the concept of God) he must also argue that man is capable of knowing God in some manner."

Mill wrote: "The rational attitude of a thinking mind toward the supernatural, whether in natural or revealed religion, is that of skepticism as distinguished from belief on one hand, and from atheism on the other ... the notion of a providential government by an omnipotent Being for the good of his creatures must be entirely dismissed ... The whole domain of the supernatural is thus removed from the region of Belief into that of simple Hope; and in that, for anything we can see, it is likely to always remain."

Because of their religious training, most people accept the fact that the world includes "things" or "beings" that are invisible. The same people, however, know where to draw the line between their vague beliefs, on one hand, and reality on the other hand. Even devoted Catholics, who believe in the reality of invisible angels and spirits acting here on Earth, can get some laughs out of "invisible reality," such as the nurse who announces to the doctor that there is an invisible man in the waiting room. "Tell him I can't see him," the doctor might joke.

Shelley said "If God has spoken, why is the world not convinced?" As Mencken has reminded us, "The most costly of all follies is to believe passionately in the palpably not true. It is the chief occupation of mankind." Einstein said "It is quite clear to me that the religious paradise of youth, which I lost, was a first attempt to free myself from the chains of the merely personal; from an existence which is dominated by wishes, hopes, and primitive feelings." Saul Bellow said "A great deal of intelligence can be invested in ignorance when the need for illusion is deep."

Oscar Wilde said "To believe is very dull. To doubt is intensely engrossing." Hume said "The Christian religion not only was at first attended with miracles, but even at this day cannot be believed by any reasonable person without one." "A man should look for what is, and not for what he thinks should be," said Einstein. George Orwell said "The Catholic and the Communist are alike in assuming that an opponent cannot be both honest and intelligent." Voltaire wrote: "Doubt is not a pleasant condition, but certainty is absurd ..." Montaigne said the same thing: "To philosophize is to doubt." Similarly, Descartes wrote that, in order to establish anything in the sciences that is stable and likely to last, a man "must abolish all his ordinary opinions, and start right from the foundations."

Religious Devotion Does Not Lead To Knowledge Or "Meaning"

If all that is true, you can study religion all your life and never have a clue about how the world really works. *From the standpoint of kings, dictators and American politicians, religion really works!* Gibbon wrote: "The evidence of the heavenly witnesses—the Father, the Word, and the Holy Ghost would now be rejected in any court of Justice."

Agnosticism Flourishes Among Well-Educated People.

According to an old Chinese proverb, "One who asks a question is a fool for a moment—but one who does not ask questions is a fool forever." Tom Paine, one of our most important Founding Fathers, said "The study of theology, as it stands in Christian churches, is the study of nothing; it is founded on nothing; it rests on no principles; it proceeds by no authorities; it has no data; it can demonstrate nothing; and it admits to no conclusion." Clarence Darrow said "I don't believe in God because I don't believe in Mother Goose." Gov. Jesse Ventura of Minnesota announced last year that organized religion is a sham and a lot of baloney. At the same time, he said that he believes that there must be a god because somebody had to create the world. Millions of Americans agree with Jesse whether they would admit it or not.

Fran Liebowitz said "If there is an afterlife, I guess I'll use it to return phone calls." Warren Buffet (no relation to Jimmy Buffet) said "The nice thing about being an agnostic is you don't think anybody is wrong." Mario Cuomo believes what most agnostics believe: "If at the end, we rejoice in what we did right and regret what we did wrong, we earn peacefulness. That's heaven. Not caring how we lived is to accept oblivion. That's Hell." On the subject of the afterlife, John Chancellor once said" I've been an agnostic for as long as I can remember … so I don't know where we go. But if it turns out that the lights are just turned off and nothing happens, well, that's OK."

Heaven Is No Longer Preferable To Life On Earth

In medieval times, when life was short and brutal, going to heaven was something people could seriously hope for. Schopenhauer wrote: "If God made the world, I would not be that God, for the misery of the world would break my heart." Today, however, particularly in an affluent place like the U.S., everyday life may be better by a long shot. Thurber said "If I have any beliefs about immortality, it is that certain dogs I have known will go to heaven, and very, very few persons." Elbert Hubbard called heaven "the Coney Island of the Christian imagination." Pascal, the French mathematician, said "God being thus hidden, any religion that does not say that God is hidden is not true, and any religion which does not explain why, does not instruct."

Each person's life has its own "meaning" and is unique. If there is no god, there is no "built-in meaning" to anything that happens in our lives. In response to a question asked by Leo Rosten about the meaning of life, Bertrand Russell answered "What is the meaning of 'the meaning of life?' I do not believe that life has a meaning; it just happens."

Where Are The Scholars Who Defend Religion?

Surely there must be some educated Christian scholars left? On the contrary, university scholars with a religious bent have nowhere to go these days. According to scholar Karen Armstrong in her book, *A History of God,* there is much to support the view that God is "dead," she says. She wrote that the Jewish theologian Richard Rubinstein "was convinced that the deity conceived as a God of History had died forever in Auschwitz." Armstrong pointed out that other Jewish theologians, such as Hans Jonas, "believed that after Auschwitz we can no longer believe in the omnipotence of God.

Armstrong summed it up as follows: "To make such human, historical phenomena as Christian 'Family Values,' 'Islam,' or 'the Holy Land' the focus of religious devotion is a new form of idolatry." Of modern "political religionists," she wrote: "They use 'God' to prop up their own loves and hates, which they attribute to God himself. But Jews, Christians, and Muslims who punctiliously attend divine services yet denigrate people who belong to different ethnic and ideological camps deny one the basic truths of their religions." God is not a Big Brother in the sky who tells us what to do, she argues. *"This image of the divine Tyrant imposing an alien law on his unwilling human servants has to go.* Terrorizing the populace into civic obedience with threats is no longer acceptable or even practical, as the downfall of communist regimes demonstrated so dramatically in the autumn of 1989."

Where does that leave most religious Americans? They are left to be exploited by the dogmatic, simplistic Christian Fundamentalists, such as Pat Robertson, Jerry Falwell, Gary Bauer, Newt Gingrich, Tammy Baker and her jailbird husband, Billy Graham and his copycat son, et al. Since the learned books of today reject Christian Fundamentalism, they have retreated to the hills and other rural areas to deliver their simplistic, *hateful* message, targeting gay people, actors, reporters, novelists, professors and scientists as the "un-American" enemy within.

Religion Is Infamous For The Harm It Has Caused

"To a philosophic eye the vices of the clergy are far less dangerous than their virtues," said Gibbon. "The most heinous and the most cruel crimes of which history has record have been committed under the cover of religion or equally noble motives," said Ghandi. Steve Allen said "No actual tyrant known to history has ever been guilty of one hundredth of the crimes, massacres, and other atrocities attributed to the Deity in the Bible."

In our own time—as shown by our daily news reporters—religion has been and is today the main cause of war, organized hatred and repression. Fanatical religionists destroyed the World Trade Center in order to make the world *better and more holy!*

Religion Does Not Make You Moral And Ethical

Most people lack the energy to follow up on interesting ideas they stumble on, like Charles Lamb, who said "Nothing puzzles me more than time and space, and yet nothing puzzles me less, for I never think about them." Churchill noticed that too: "Men occasionally stumble over the truth, but most of them pick themselves up and hurry off as if nothing had happened." Andrew Carnegie said, "I don't believe in God. My God is patriotism. Teach a man to be a good citizen and you have solved the problem of life." Here's an old saying about all that: "A truly good person is not someone who prays, but someone who can sell his parrot to the town gossip without moving away."

Religion Has Always Abused Its Power And Caused Harm

Historians can tell you that the Roman Catholic Church, during a period of almost a thousand years, committed the greatest recorded crimes against humanity, many of them so cruel, obscene and disgusting that Hitler's holocaust looks benign, if that is imaginable, in order to make examples of "heretics" (ie., innocent, uneducated people who could not or did not conform to the rules of the Church). See, for example, *The Perfect Heresy*, by Stephen O'Shea. What rational person can excuse god for such horrors? "The only excuse for god is that he doesn't exist," said Stendhal. H.L. Mencken said "To die for an idea it is unquestionably noble. But how much nobler it would be if men died for ideas that were true!" Winston Churchill said "No folly is more costly than the folly of intolerant idealism." Erasmus said "I don't see by what right we send a priest to the flames who prefers the wife to the concubine." Thomas Hardy summed it up concisely: "God, but not religion: good." Daniel Defoe said "And of all plagues with which mankind are cursed, Ecclesiastic tyranny's the worst." Tennyson wrote: "There lives more faith in honest doubt, Believe me, than in half the creeds."

A recent book that deals with the bad side of religion is *Papal Sins*, by Gary Wills, a prominent Catholic layman. He says at the outset that the Church has cleaned up its act significantly, to the point where it no longer routinely amasses personal fortunes; no longer is willing to murder, torture and conquer for secular, political purposes; no longer has sexual scandals that match those of the papal bastards who once ran its vast, corrupt bureaucracy; no longer condones teenaged popes who die in the beds of married women, etc. Wills is only

concerned with current problems such as historical dishon-
esties (ignoring the Holocaust); hypocritically opposing birth
control; excluding women from the priesthood; forbidding marriage to priests (because of the delicate problem of "clerical mistresses" in Italy and other countries); covering up child
molestation and homosexuality in the priesthood, which is
now making headlines in our daily papers; taking inconsistent
positions on whether a fetus is a person; hiding authentic
church documents to avoid criticism; fostering censorship
everywhere; ignoring political manipulation, dishonesty and
deception inside the Vatican; and doctrinal inconsistencies, etc.
*With a history that bad" wh*at *good could religion do?* Is Wills a
Catholic-basher? (Most Catholics I know would say that such
histories are just lies! That is why they are not agnostics.)

"Christianity must be divine," said Voltaire, "since it has
lasted seventeen hundred years despite the fact that it's full of
villainy and nonsense." For example, The original Pope John
XXII was deposed for "notorious incest, adultery, defilement,
homicide, and theft." While still a chamberlain, he had openly
kept his brother's wife as a mistress. While a cardinal in
Bologna, "two hundred maids, matrons, and widows, including
a few nuns, fell victim to his brutal lust." Pope Innocent VII
was nicknamed "the Honest," because he was the first pope to
acknowledge his illegitimate children publicly. ("I would have
made a good pope," said Nixon.)

Father Valdemar, a priest in Toledo, Spain, was found
guilty of rape, blasphemy, consorting with prostitutes, and
extorting the favors of a young woman. He was sentenced to a
30-day house arrest and a fine of only two ducats, presumably
because his offense was considered commonplace. Pope Paul IV,
who carried out the Inquisition, ordered the removal of
Michaelangelo's paintings from the Sistine Chapel on the
ground that they were "obscene." His pupil was ordered to add
clothes to all the naked figures (including all the angels and the

Virgin Mary) in The Last Judgment, after which he was nick-named "the pants-maker."

Simone Weil wrote: "All conceptions of God which are incompatible with the movement of pure charity are false." JeanPaul Marat said "God has always been hard on the poor." *On the whole, religion has not been good for people in general. The Catholic church has traditionally opposed all new developments in the arts and sciences, including, for example, printing and the wide distribution of books (including Bibles!).* If the Church had had its way, ordinary people still would not be permitted to read the Bible without a religious tutor.

Agnosticism Is Everywhere

Agnosticism is often viewed as something odd because it is not popular and well-organized like "other religions." In fact, agnosticism relates only to a person's individual conscience and is not similar to a religion or any "movement." In any large city or sophisticated locale, such as a college campus, the sidewalks are full of agnostics walking along like everybody else. Ambrose Beirce, the 19th century's most famous journalist, defined "irreligion" as "The principal one of the great faiths of the world," meaning that agnosticism is as important and as widespread as any particular religious faith.

All we can do, religionists say, is pray to god and *try* to understand him as best we can with our eternally limited knowledge. They are right that "knowledge" is what this is all about. At the same time, however, church leaders then tell us what god wants us to do in everyday life! They say he does not want us to use profanity, take drugs, gamble, drink booze, watch sex videos or play golf on Sunday mornings!

The Founding Fathers Were Agnostic

As discussed in Chapter 8, America's Founding Fathers and early Presidents were agnostic, their support of religion being limited to the concept that someone ("god") *probably* created the universe. They did not, however, believe in the Bible or in an active god who micromanages everything that happens in the world and listens to individual prayers. Jefferson even published his own version of the Bible that omits all miracles and magical things; a copy of the Jefferson Bible is located at the U.S Congress.

Faith Is Relied Upon Only Because God Cannot Be Known

"We may define 'faith' as a firm belief in something for which there is no evidence," said Russell. "Faith can move mountains, but not furniture," said Eric Hoffer, the longshoreman philosopher. "Faith may be defined briefly as an illogical belief in the occurrence of the improbable," wrote Mencken. George Smith wrote: "*... the Christian wishes to claim as knowledge beliefs that have not been (and often cannot be) rationally demonstrated, so he posits faith as an alternative method of acquiring knowledge.*" Since acquiring faith does not increase one's supply of knowledge one bit (but probably *reduces* one's store of knowledge by denying what is in fact known about the universe), faith is simply irrelevant to the factual, actual world we live in.

Many of the most educated Americans, like the late University of North Carolina professor Mortimer Adler, wanted to believe that god exists but could not make a reasonable argument to support that.

The Christian view of history, human nature and the physical world is not taught in any of America's accredited colleges and universities. Why is that? It is because religion is contrary to reality. That is why, of course, Christian Fundamentalists want to put prayer back in the classroom! Miguel de Unamuno said "Faith is in its essence simply a matter of will, not of reason, and to believe is to wish to believe, and to believe in God is, before all and above all, to wish that there may be a God." Galileo said "I do not feel obliged to believe that the same God who has endowed us with sense, reason, and intellect has intended us to forgo their use."

Maxwell Anderson said "The Gods of men are sillier than their kings and queens, and emptier and more powerless." Religion, of course, also exists outside of churches dedicated to mainstream religion. Millions of Americans in recent years say religion is best practiced outside of church, because churches are so inflexible and repressive. Jello Biafra of the Dead Kennedys said "If you love God, burn a church."

The Existence Of God Is Now A Political Matter

A majority of ignorant people in any jurisdiction can vote to teach the Bible in schools, but that does not establish the truth of religion or change the facts of life, such as geology, astronomy, botany, biology, etc. Noam Chomsky, a leading American philosopher, wrote: "It is well known that belief in the Bible is concentrated among the poorest and most poorly educated people in the U. S. Politicians work this angle every election year. In those areas neither major party ever runs a nonreligious candidate. "Religious fundamentalists alone are a huge popular grouping in the United States, which resembles preindustrial societies in that regard. *This is a culture in which three-fourths of the population believe in religious miracles, half believe in the devil, 83 percent believe that the Bible is the 'actual' or the inspired word of God, 39 percent believe in the Biblical prediction of Armageddon and accept it with a certain fatalism,' a mere 9 percent accept Darwinian evolution while 44 percent believe that 'God created man pretty much in his present form at one time within the last 10,000 years,' and so on."*

Robert Hutchins said "One thing you learn very quickly in teaching students at the loftiest levels of education is that they cannot read." (If you have got this far in this book, you may be okay.)

Obviously, there is a great gap in America between what our foremost thinkers know and what our high school and college graduates believe. Christianity Is Incompatible With Contemporary Culture.

In any case, the message of Jesus, as reported in the Bible, is not relevant to American civilization. "If Jesus Christ were to come today, people would not even crucify him. They would ask him to dinner, and hear what he had to say, and make fun of it," said Carlyle. He also said "Just in the ratio knowledge increases, faith decreases." Christianity thrives best among uneducated people, which is why the Fundamentalists say the Bible is the only book you'll ever need. In Christian colleges, students get only "Christian" books to read! Robert Carr, of Lamprey Systems, said "That's why the religious people are so freaked out about the Internet, not because of the smut but because NO religion can stand up to access to information." Welcome to the club. Believing in god is basically selfish, self-centered and timid.

Leo Tolstoy said "Freethinkers are those who are willing to use their minds without prejudice and without fearing to understand things that clash with their own customs, privileges, or beliefs. This state of mind is not common, but is essential for valid thinking; where it is absent, discussion is apt to become worse than useless." Josh Billings, an American humorist, said "It is better to know nothing than to know what ain't so."

Ignorance And Apathy Support Religion.

Harvard professor Stephen Jay Gould, America's most popular scientific writer in recent years, said "I am not a believer. I am an agnostic in the wise sense of Huxley, who coined the word in identifying such open-minded skepticism as the only rational position because, truly, one cannot know." Freud wrote: "The more the fruits of knowledge became accessible to man, the more widespread is the decline of religious belief." Higher education, especially, always weakens religion. "It was here (at Oxford) that I suspended my religious studies," said the historian Edward Gibbon. "It must be remembered that we have heard only one side of the case. God has written all the books," said Samuel Butler, before books were widely distributed.

On the other hand, some clever person said just changing your religion or shopping around for another god is like marrying your mistress (or your boyfriend), which just creates a job vacancy and doesn't change your situation at all. J.B.S. Haldane wrote: "I've never met a really healthy person who worried much about his health, or a really good person who worried much about his soul."

Christianity gives us all "original sin" when we are born, like a fly in our soup every day. It also puts a fly in the ointment we use to heal. God, in other words, has an endless supply of dead flies to make us unhappy with life on Earth and long for heaven, where presumably there is soup and ointment without flies. (Imagine one angel speaking to another angel, peeping down at some Earthlings. "I've got one more fly left for today, and they're going across the street for dessert now!") Today, of course, optimism is in and pessimism is out, at least in the business and political community, which is one more reason why Christianity has had its day. "What time has been wasted during man's destiny / In the struggle to decide what man's next world will be like / The keener the effort to find out, the less he knew about the present one he lived in ..." said Sean O'Casey, one of Ireland's two world-class intellectuals.

We all know deeply religious people whose daily lives are wasted completely. Marcus Aurelius, a second century Roman emperor, wrote that, whether there is a god or not, human beings will get along just the same: "Either there is a God and all is well; or, if all things go by chance and fortune, yet mayest thou use thine own providence in those things that concern thee properly, and then art thou well."

A song by Phil Ochs goes: "And I won't be laughing at the lies when I'm gone / And I can't question how or when or why when I'm gone / Can't live proud enough to die when I'm gone / So I guess I'll have to do it while I'm here." Will Rogers, a down-to-earth guy, said "Extreme traditionalists live a large part of their lives in the past because they dislike what is going on around them. Don't let yesterday use up too much of today." There are many persons who look on Sunday as a sponge to wipe out the sins of the week," said Henry Ward Beecher.

So: you are already an agnostic. The real question then becomes: are you an atheist? As Casey Stengel used to say about baseball history and statistics: "You could look it up!" Baseball stats are not controversial, and neither are stats about the Earth and the rest of the universe.

GOD'S APATHY

CHAPTER 2

ATHEISM

"An atheist is a man who watches a Notre Dame—Southern Methodist game and doesn't care who wins."
—Dwight D. Eisenhower

Unlike an agnostic, an atheist has come to the firm conclusion, after investigating it, that neither he nor anyone else can have knowledge of god, *and that god is not part of human reality.* The difference between an agnostic and an atheist is like the difference between (a) a 250-pound woman who *thinks* her bikini may be two small for her and (b) a 250-pound woman who *knows* her bikini is too small for her. It is, after all, a question of common sense; the bikini either covers the matter or it does not.

Some commentators, however (such as Sloan Gary), take the position that agnosticism and atheism are essentially the same: "The term 'atheist' may be correctly applied to anyone who doesn't believe supernatural entities exist. According to this definition, those who equate god with the totality of nature, as did Baruch Spinoza, Giordano Bruno, Walt Whitman and Albert Einstein, are atheists. So are agnostics: fence-sitting doesn't constitute belief," said Gary.

"An atheist is a man with no invisible means of support," said John Buchan. "Atheism is "heresy," which, according to Graham Greene, "is only another word for freedom of thought." Philip K. Dick wrote: "Reality is that which, when you stop believing in it, doesn't go away." Voltaire defined "atheist" as: "A name given by theologians to whoever differs from them in their ideas concerning the divinity, or who refuse to believe in it in the form of which, in the emptiness of their infallible pates, they have resolved to present it to him. As a rule an atheist is any or every man who does not believe in the God of the priests."

In any case, atheism is not an organization or a movement; it is a "non-prophet" organization. You cannot become an atheist by persuasion or indoctrination, like a communist, or a Catholic. It is the state of being independent and "self-directed" as a matter of will. Atheists believe in a mechanical, accidental world. According to Jay Leno: "The atheists have produced a Christmas play, called "Coincidence on 34th Street."

During and after World War II, a form of atheism called "Existentialism" swept the universities of Europe and greatly influenced American thought. Its principal founder, Jean-Paul Sartre, said that, since there is no god, each person must acquire a new way of looking at the world in which each person has the burden of developing a philosophy of life sufficiently strong to replace the concept of god. He said: "Existence is prior to essence," meaning that personal subjectivity must be the starting point of philosophy, and that the human individual— not something outside the human being—is the central concern of all legitimate philosophical thinking.

According to *Who's Who in Hell*, Pascal, St. Augustine, Socrates, Karl Jaspers, Miguel de Unimuno, and Norman

Mailer have been associated with Existentialism. So have theologians Barth, Buber, Bultmann, Kierkegaard and Tillich. Existentialism centers on individual humans who are tying to live out their lives in an unfathomable universe, one in which they, with free will, must try to determine without certainty what is right or wrong or good or bad. Sartre was indebted to Kierkegaard, who asserted that "all essential knowledge relates to existence, or only such knowledge as has an essential relationship to existence is essential knowledge." In other words, truth and knowledge are not things "out there" but things in our own brains that deal with ourselves and the actual world. "Existentialism means that nobody can take a bath for you," said Delmore Schwartz: we have to run our own lives. (Or, your church or synagogue will run it.)

Believers in god argue that somebody had to create the world because otherwise there would be "nothingness." Imagine Sartre sitting at a French cafe revising his first draft of *Being and Nothingness.* He says to the waitress, "I'd like a cup of coffee, please, with no cream." The waitress replies, "I'm sorry, monsieur, but we're out of cream. How about with no milk?" Religionists, of course, have no problem here: they think "nothingness" once *existed*, like the 1950 Plymouth your father once owned. How can nothingness "exist"? There is no thing in the universe that is by definition "nothing."

Charles Bukowski said "For those who believe in God, most of the big questions are answered. But for those of us who can't readily accept the God formula, the big answers don't remain stone-written. We adjust to new conditions and discoveries. We are pliable. Love needs not a command, or faith a dictum. I am my own God. We are here to unlearn the teachings of the church, state, and our education system. We are here to drink beer. We are here to kill war. We are here to laugh at the odds and live our lives so well that Death will tremble to take us."

Likewise, Rance Van Ducy said "When did I realize that I

was master of my own destiny ... that I was my own god? Well, I was praying and suddenly realized I was talking too myself." Justin Brown asked "If the Bible is mistaken in telling us where we came from, how can we trust it to tell us where we're going?" Dan Barker, a former preacher, wrote: "I am an atheist because there is no evidence for the existence of God. That should be all that needs to be said about it: no evidence, no belief." On the subject of human freedom, Bakunin wrote: "If God is, man is a slave; now, man can and must be free; then, God does not exist. I defy anyone whomsoever to avoid this circle; now, therefore, let all choose." George Santayana, a leading 20th century philosopher, explained it this way: "My atheism, like that of Spinoza, is true piety toward the universe and denies only gods fashioned by men in their own image."

Probably, the best-known American atheist was Madelyn O'Hair, who became famous for winning a federal court case upholding her Constitutional right be a citizen and an atheist at the same time (which is still applicable to everybody except our Attorney General, John Ashcroft, who believes it is incorrect). O'Hair said "An atheist says to you: "What you see is what you get." According to the newspapers, she was robbed, murdered and dismembered by a devout Christian (who, theoretically at least, should now be in heaven).

George Smith wrote: "... atheism, as such, is not an answer to anything, but it provides a general context in which answers are possible. Atheism provides one with a clean slate, in effect, and what one does beyond this point is entirely a matter of choice.

But under no circumstances should atheism be regarded as a cure-all or as an escape from personal responsibility."

You Are Already An Experienced Atheist!

That, of course, is how most Americans still think today, in the year 2002: *they are atheists about all religions in the world (except their own) because those other religions are irrational!* Stephen Roberts said "I contend that we are both atheists. I just believe in one fewer god than you do. When you understand why you dismiss all the other possible gods, you will understand why I dismiss yours." You dismiss other gods because your parents told you that their god is the only god, and all other gods are just a figment of imagination. *You understand clearly that most gods are merely figments of imagination, but you have not even made any kind of investigation in the question of the one your parents picked for you.*

On the other hand: *"The equal toleration of all religions … is the same as atheism,"* said Pope Leo XIII. If that is true as a principle, you should tolerate atheism the same way you tolerate Judaism or Islam! If the religionists are right, some day god is going to name the one true religion, which will be a crushing blow to almost everybody in the world. The Pope, of course, will call a meeting of all the Cardinals and say "I have good news and bad news. The good news is that I just talked to Jesus. He has been resurrected, so our faith in his existence has been justified! The bad news is he was calling from Salt Lake City."

We have at least reached the point where normal people (meaning those other than Christian Fundamentalist demagogues) can at least make good jokes about atheism, such as this popular one: "They have Dial-a-Religion for atheists. When you call, nobody answers." The U.S. Statistical Survey lists "atheism" as a "religious denomination" with almost zero "membership," apparently on the theory that the only atheists are those few thousand who belong to nationwide atheist organizations. Under the theory that atheism is a religion, Paula Poundstone imagined it like this: "In an atheist church they also have crippled guys who stand up and say they were once crippled—but here they still are."

Bullfinch, in his famous 19th century work entitled

Mythology, which was the most popular source of knowledge about myths and legends, etc., for over a hundred years, said this about the subject of ancient Greek religion: "The creation of the world is a problem naturally fitted to excite the liveliest interest of man, its inhabitant. *The ancient pagans, not having the information on the subject which we derive from the pages of Scripture,* had their own way of telling the story, which is as follows ..." That shows that Bullfinch was intelligent enough to see that religions are myths, but not intelligent enough (or courageous enough) to see that his own religion is also a myth!

There are many people who think that atheists are in some kind of a struggle *only against a particular god.* Quentin Crisp reported that "When I told the people of Northern Ireland that I was an atheist, a woman in the audience stood up and said, "Yes, but is it the God of the Catholics or the God of the Protestants in whom you don't believe?"

Atheism Is Not A "Movement" But A State Of Mind

Our current Bush President said that "atheists should not be considered patriots, or even citizens. This is one nation under God, damn it!" He is obviously not aware of the First Amendment to the Constitution, or else believes it can be ignored. He has also said "Now don't get me wrong, folks, the Muslims and Jews are gonna burn in hell forever, along with everyone else who doesn't believe in Jesus." Thus he is either (a) dishonest because he tells uneducated voters what they want to hear, however stupid, or (b) he is himself very uneducated, as he has several times admitted (having drunk his way through Yale on the connections of his father and grandfather).

Christians believe that, because our lives are so "short" (compared to eternity), there can be no point to them, or that there can be a point to a short life only if there is an afterlife! As Steven Wright joked: "Our birth certificates would all have expiration dates."

Current University Scholarship

University scholars overwhelmingly reject all arguments for the existence of a god. As a result, religious leaders have abandoned all pretenses of a "debate" with secular university scholars, who consist mainly of agnostics and atheists. Flew starts his inquiry about god this way: "How could we identify the Being so specified? Until and unless this can be answered there can be no question of existence or of non-existence." *That is to say, unless we can describe god, it is pretty hard to say he exists.* He said "... God has got to be an individual; albeit, of course, an unique and the supreme individual ... This in turn means that it has got to be shown how what is specified in our definition of the word God could, in principle, be identified. ... Before I can be called on to believe a statement on the authority of the Church or the Scriptures, it is necessary to give me sufficient reasons for accepting the Church or the Scripture as declaring the mind of God ..."

Surely, if god expected his creatures to follow his rules, he would have made those rules clear to all mankind. "It will not do at all," Flew wrote, "to proclaim in elaborate detail God's will with regard to all manner of intimate or public human affairs, and then, when hard-pressed with questions about the nature of this God of yours, to maintain that it is shrouded in inscrutable mystery." Yet, of course, that is exactly what the preachers, rabbis and priests do all the time! He said "Only if there *is* a God do any questions arise about the irrationality or incoherence of what must then be seen as his doings. Hence it is preposterous to wish on to the atheist any such desperate cosmological views." In other words, the existence of god cannot be proven by the existence of the world itself. Karl Popper, a pre-eminent Austrian-British philosopher of the twentieth century, said "That which cannot at least in principle be known by the method of science cannot be known ..." Some scientists use the term "god" to refer to the principles underlying the way the universe works, rather than to a "diety" above and beyond the universe. Although some people are confused by that terminology, it does not mean that god must exist because certain principles and "rules" underlie nature. That is like saying that god exists because $2+2=4$. (For example, see "God in the Equation" by Corey Powell.) Most mainline scientific philosophers regard it as just a colorful way of referring to scientific findings about how the world actually works, rather than any kind of discovery or proof of god's existence. The fact that the universe is not pure chaos does not prove that a god created it. It may well be, scientists tell us, that pure chaos is impossible. (See Chapter 6.) Einstein asked this question: "How is it possible to think of holding men responsible for their deeds and thoughts before such an almighty Being? In giving out punishments and rewards he would be to a certain extent passing judgment on himself."

Emerson wrote: "Other world? There is no other world! Here or nowhere is the whole fact." Vonnegut said "Say what you will about the sweet miracle of unquestioning faith. I consider the capacity for it terrifying." Howard Stern said "I'm sickened by all religions. Religion has divided people. I don't think there's any difference between the pope wearing a large hat and parading around with a smoking purse and an African painting his face white and praying to a rock." Sinclair Lewis said "Religion has caused more misery to all men in every state of human history than any other single idea." Ex-preacher Dan Barker also wrote: "The very concept of sin comes from the bible. Christianity offers to solve a problem of its own making! Would you be thankful to a person who cut you with a knife in order to sell you a bandage?"

Atheism Rejects "Predestination" And "God's Fate"

According to Flew, god is either "the Supreme Puppetmaster with creatures whose every thought and move he arranges; or ... the Great Hypnotist with subjects who always act out of his irresistible suggestions. This precisely means that absolutely nothing happens save by his ultimate, undetermined determination ... Everything means everything: and that includes every human thought, every human action, and every human choice."

Thus, says Flew, a fundamental reason for being atheistic is to reject the Christian view that everything in life is predestined. *In short: if creation is in, autonomy is out,* wrote Flew. He says, "predestination is the immediate consequence of basic theism." Faced with this impeccable logic, how could an intelligent person not consider atheism? Any serious, logical study of Christianity could only lead to atheism.

For example, the Church of England holds "that the whole course of events is under the control of God ... logically this involves the affirmation that there is no event, and no aspect of any event, even those due to sin ... which falls outside the scope of his purposive activity. Thoughtful, independent people simply find that idea unacceptable because it makes a mockery of all human decisions. *There is no point to life at all if everything we do is willed by god.* That means, inevitably, that nothing matters! We are not responsible! Trying to be moral is hopeless! Democracy is meaningless! Laws against crime are meaningless! But we can't have it both ways: if god created us and sustains the world he created, we are puppets, said Flew. "If in fact we ever are free agents, and this is in a sense which is incompatible with being completely the creatures of a creator, then what follows is ... that there cannot be any Creator at all."

According to Flew, it would be inconsistent to say that god is both the infinitely powerful creator and yet possesses a will which his creatures can, and regularly do, disobey (unless, of course, god *expects* us to disobey and take our punishment). That means that disobedience and punishment are unavoidable, which is certainly a sign of an imperfect, if not vindictive, creator. Either way, life is meaningless! Quoting Piaget, a leading twentieth century Swiss philosopher, Flew said "Only in theology ... does the idea of Original Sin keep alive the notion of collective responsibility; Adam's fall leaves on the whole of humanity a stain that calls for expiation. In law and in ethics such ideas would revolt us." (Piaget's principal theory was that humans are born without any logical faculties, which they eventually construct themselves through their experiences with the world—which of course rules out original sin.) Some jokester said "Nobody ever inferred from the multiple infirmities of Windows 95 that Bill Gates was infinitely benevolent, omniscient, and willing to fix it for nothing."

E.M. Forster summed up the Christian inconsistency about determinism and original sin as follows: "One has two duties—to be worried and not to be worried. The doctrine of original sin, which holds that *humans are all born as sinners whether they actually sinned or not,* is so psychologically damaging to healthy people that they simply do not accept it any more." Joseph Lewis said "I do not believe that if there is a God of this vast universe that such a God would create a hell to torment to all eternity helpless and innocent human beings." Robert Browning wrote: "Life is pointless, because we are not in control: All service ranks the same with God, whose puppets, best and worst, we are: there is no last nor first."

Flew agrees with Browning: *human life is meaningless if we are puppets! That means god makes us do bad things and then punishes us for it!* Ignazio Silone said "Destiny is an invention of the cowardly and the resigned." Professor Pinker said "Believers ... don't pause to wonder why a God who knows our intentions has to listen to your prayers, or how a God can both see into the future and care about how we choose to act ..." Vonnegut said "Say what you will about the sweet miracle of unquestioning faith. I consider the capacity for it terrifying."

Sinclair Lewis said "Religion has caused more misery to all men in every state of human history than any other single idea."

Natalie Angier said "So I'll out myself. I'm an atheist. I don't believe in God, gods, godlets or any sort of higher power beyond the universe itself, which seems quite high and powerful enough to me. I don't believe in life after death, channeled chat rooms with the dead, reincarnation, telekinesis or any miracles but the miracle of life and consciousness, which again strike me as miracles in nearly obscene abundance. I believe that the universe abides by the laws of physics ..." Flannery O'Connor wrote: "I'm going to preach there was no Fall because there was nothing to fall from, and no Redemption because there was no Fall, and no Judgment because there wasn't the first two. Nothing matters but that Jesus was a liar." Carl Sagan said "I would love to believe that when I die I will live again, that some thinking, feeling, remembering part of me will continue. But as much as I want to believe that, and despite the ancient and worldwide cultural traditions that assert an afterlife, I know of nothing to suggest that it is more than wishful thinking."

Organized Religion Opposes Atheism Out Of Ignorance.

In order to protect "decency" and "Americanism," people lie about atheism all the time. Wendy Kaminer wrote: "America's pluralistic ideal does not protect atheism; public support for different belief systems is matched by intolerance of disbelief. According to surveys published in the early 1980s, before today's millennial religious revivalism, nearly 70 percent of all Americans agreed that the freedom to worship "applies to all religious groups, regardless of how extreme their beliefs are; but only 26 percent agreed that the freedom of atheists to make fun of God and religion "should be legally protected no matter who might be offended." Seventy-one percent held that atheists "who preach against God and religion" should not be permitted to use civic auditoriums. Intolerance for atheism was stronger even than intolerance of homosexuality.

The Death-of-God Movement

In the 1960s, prominent religious leaders developed what is now called "radical theology," which, for all practical purposes, is a "religion" *without* an all powerful god who runs things. (It was a movement of religious leaders, not a movement of atheists or agnostics.) In *The Gospel of Christian Atheism*, Thomas J. Altizer, a professor of religion at Emory University, claimed that the "good news" of god's death "has freed us from slavery to a tyrannical transcendent deity. For obvious reasons, a benevolent and wise God could not have deliberately created the human misery that has always existed ... Every time he causes a volcano to erupt or a river to overrun its banks or an earthquake to destroy buildings, he kills thousands of innocent children and worthy human beings."

They said that the Bible is meaningless because everything in it is open to interpretation. In their book, *Radical Theology and the Death of God*, Altizer and Hamilton write that "... there is no God and there never has been," and ... "That the Christian story is no longer a saving or a healing story." Paul Van Buren, a religious writer, claimed that "it is no longer possible to speak of God acting in the world ... Science and technology have made the old mythology invalid. A simple faith in the Old Man in the Sky is now clearly impossible, but so has been the more sophisticated beliefs of the theologians." Thus, they argued, we must do without god and hold on to Jesus as a real human person of great moral stature. The Gospel, said a religious writer named Paul Van Buren, is "the good news of a free man who has set other men free." They see Jesus as a sort of "holy man" on Earth.

Altizer and Hamilton, who have been called "Christian atheists," also wrote: "It is an attempt to set an atheist point of view within the spectrum of Christian possibilities." They wrote: "That certain concepts of God, often in the past confused with the classical Christian doctrine of God, must be destroyed, for example, God as problem-solver, absolute power, necessary being, the object of ultimate concern," ... and that men today do not experience God except as hidden, absent and silent.

Similarly, Hamilton said "I do not see how preaching, worship, prayer, ordination, the sacraments can be taken seriously by the radical theologian." In *A History of God*, Karen Armstrong wrote "An omnipotent, all-knowing tyrant is not so different from earthly dictators who made everything and everybody mere cogs in the machine which they controlled. An atheism that rejects such a God is amply justified." Van Buren claimed that "it is no longer possible to speak of God acting in the world ... Science and technology have made the old mythology invalid."

Einstein asked this question: "How is it possible to think of holding men responsible for their deeds and thoughts before such an almighty Being? In giving out punishments and rewards he would be to a certain extent passing judgment on himself." If god runs the world, he is responsible for its evil. God makes you sin for the sole purpose of punishing you in hell.

God Is Used To Justify War And Evil

Today, god is on the side of Osama Bin Laden, the Afghanistanis, the Syrians, the Saudis, the Iraquis, the Iranis, the Pakistanis, the Palestinians, the right-wing Jews in Israel and the Serbs and Kosovars, etc. God's record in picking sides is, of course, a losing one. Armstrong also said: "They use 'God' to prop up their own loves and hates, which they attribute to God himself ... . *This image of the divine Tyrant imposing an alien law on his unwilling human servants has to go.*"

Certainly Christianity is a failure if the acts of Christians are the test. "My luck is getting worse and worse," said Woody Allen. "Last night, for instance, I was mugged by a Quaker." John Lennon said "Christianity will go. It will vanish and shrink. I needn't argue with that; I'm right and I will be proved right. We're more popular than Jesus now; I don't know which will go first—rock and roll or Christianity."

Allan Bloom, a professor of philosophy, wrote in his best-seller, *The Closing of the American Mind*: "Millenia of philosophizing about the soul had resulted in no certitude about it, while those who pretended to know, the priests, held power or influence and corrupted politics as a result. Princes were rendered ineffective by their own or their subjects' opinions about the salvation of their souls, while men slaughtered each other wholesale because of differences of such opinion. The care of the soul crippled men in the conduct of their lives."

Schopenhauer said "The bad thing about all religions is that, instead of being able to confess their allegorical nature, they have to conceal it; accordingly, they parade their doctrine in all seriousness as true sensu proprio [reality], and as absurdities form an essential part of these doctrines, you have the great mischief of a continual fraud." Conrad said: "The belief in a supernatural source of evil is not necessary; men alone are quite capable of every wickedness."

Tolstoy wrote: "But Christ could certainly not have established the Church. That is, the institution we now call by that name, for nothing resembling our present conception of the Church—with its sacraments, its hierarchy, and especially its claim to infallibility—is to be found in Christ's words or in the conception of the men of his time … *In the periodical absolution of sins at Confession I see a harmful deception which only encourages immorality and causes men not to fear to sin* … Free-thinkers are those who are willing to use their minds without prejudice and without fearing to understand things that clash with their own customs, privileges, or beliefs. This state of mind is not common, but it is essential for right thinking; where it is absent, discussion is apt to become worse than useless."

Tolstoy also warned us as follows: "All the philosophers of the world who had a religion have said in all ages: "There is a God; and one must be just. That, then, is the universal religion established in all ages and throughout mankind. The point in which they all agree is therefore true, and the systems through which they differ therefore false ... Anyone who has the power to make you believe absurdities has the power to make you commit injustices. Needless to say, since Christ's expiation, not one single Christian has been known to sin, or die."

Extremely devout (guilty) people accuse themselves of sins at the confessional even if they in fact have committed no sins at all, which is certainly not mentally healthy. (A priest once remarked that hearing confessions of nuns is like "being stoned to death with popcorn.") Christians do not live in the real world.

In *Many Worlds*, a compilation of contemporary knowledge concerning science and religion edited by Steven J. Dick, a contemporary British theoretical physicist named Paul C. W. Davies had this to say about the death of god: "It is meant to imply that the God we invented two thousand years ago is no longer compatible with what we know about the world." He said that "life is an information processing and propagating system," and agrees with the views of Monod and Gould that atheism is what results from the scenario that life and intelligence are freak accidents, unique in the cosmos.

Davies quotes Monod's statement that "Man at last knows that he is alone in the unfeeling immensity of the universe, out of which he has emerged only by chance." Another contributor to Dick's book, Arthur Peacocke (an Anglican priest as well as a scientist), wrote that the Christian god is "obsolete in relation to the reality of life today," and that "a new kind of theology must be developed that is consistent with the scientific view of the universe." Many religionists today, including Peacocke, take the position that god must be present in nature, if he exists at all, and therefore is part of evolution itself. He wrote: "Any theology, any attempt to relate God to all-that-is, will be moribund and doomed if it does not incorporate this perspective into its very bloodstream. Yet much Christian theology simply tinkers apologetically with its beliefs at what seem vulnerable chinks in its armor, hoping that it will survive into what it hopes will be less challenging times. That is a recipe for extinction for it with this evolving world that on the surface of planet Earth the tragicomedy of human existence is working itself out. We are part of nature, part of an evolving cosmos, indeed, we are stardust become persons!"

The Question Of Evil And God's Benevolence

"God was good on the physical and emotional sides and a great one for hate," wrote Anthony Burgess. "He generously spilled his own hate into his dearest creation." As reported by Voltaire, Fr. Jean Meslier, Cure' d'Etrepigny, France, wrote: "It is absurd to call him a God of justice and goodness, who inflicts evil indiscriminately on the good and the wicked, upon the innocent and the guilty. *It is idle to demand that the unfortunate should console themselves for their misfortunes in the very arms of the one who alone is the author of them.*" Joseph Lewis said "Man's inhumanity to man will continue as long as man loves God more than he loves his fellow man."

If god is all powerful, he is responsible for evil, says Flew. "Now some Christians have perhaps been blatantly and from the beginning worshippers of infinite power as such … To the extent, of course, that you are really prepared to do this there can for you be no Problem of Evil." That is, you must accept evil as a feature of god's pure power. Flew also wrote … "there are

many evils which it scarcely seems either are or could be reme-
died in this way: animal suffering, for instance." In any case,
the creation of evil by god makes no sense, says Flew: "... even
if you can show room for saying that all actual evils do in fact
serve as the material for a logically higher order good, you have
not thereby shown that everything will be, or could be, for the
best. The price could still be too high ... Is it really worth having injuries in order to have acts of forgiveness, or worth having suffering in order to have exercises in fortuities? Or, does
evil arise from man's own freedom? God gave us this precious
freedom, and look how—no fault of his—we wickedly abuse it.
This move still leaves a good deal of evil unaccounted for," says
Flew, meaning that god must cause everything we do not cause,
no matter how bad or evil we are. "The possibility of affirming,
and praising, God's goodness depends on the possibility of recognizing, and condemning, the evils of the world," Flew said.
*Thus if you want to say that god is good, you have to accept evil
as caused by god, which is irrational.*

But the Christian truth is even worse! Pius XII reminded
us that: ... "the Supreme Judge, in His last judgment, applies
uniquely the principle of retribution ...," meaning that a
Christian is bound, even reluctantly, *"to concede that your God
creates some creatures intending to subject them to eternal tor-
ments ..."* According to the Bible, god is a tyrant who strikes
down people without any qualms. The world we live in, with all
its evil, is therefore the world of god if there is a god, who
"created" evil as something for people to struggle against! *An
atheist can rationally attempt to solve or ameliorate those ca-
tastrophes, but a Christian cannot change a vengeful god.*

According to *Who's Who in Hell*, edited by Warren Allen
Smith, George Carlin described religion as follows: "When it
comes to bullshit—big-time, major-league bullshit—you have
to stand in awe of the all-time champion of false promises and
exaggerated claims: religion ... Religion has actually convinced

people that there's an invisible man, living in the sky, who watches everything you do," he joked, a man who "has a special list of ten things he does not want you to do—and if you do any of these ten things, he has a special place full of fire and smoke and burning and torture and anguish where he will send you to live and suffer and burn and choke and scream and cry forever and ever till the end of time. But He *loves* you."

There Is No Evidence Of God That Can Be Examined

Descartes based his philosophy on the proposition that if you don't *think*, you don't exist: "I think, therefore I am." That insight, not the presumed existence of god (something outside of himself), was the foundation of his work. (Philosophy students joke that this could backfire: Descartes is sitting in a bar, having a drink. The bartender asks him if he would like another. "I think not," he says, which makes him vanish.)

A.J. Ayer, an eminent twentieth century British "logical positivist" philosopher, argued that religious claims "are devoid of cognitive meaning," which is a scholarly way of saying they are *meaningless because they do not correspond to anything in the physical world*. "Practically all philosophers of any intellectual eminence are openly or secretly freethinkers," said Russell. Similarly, Goethe said a long time ago "What we do not understand, we do not possess," such as, for example, knowledge of how god runs the world. Since accurate historical records have been kept, has god ever intervened to do anything *good*?

The Herd Instinct Supports Religion Today

Many people continue to oppose atheism because they are afraid god might exist, or they are simply illogical people, or they are afraid to associate with atheists. Here is how they think: since so many people believe that god exists, it is probable that god does exist! Can millions of people be wrong? *Yes!* "I believe in god because everybody around me can't be wrong!"

If they don't like what the doctor says, they read the Bible. That is like buying another newspaper, hoping the sun will shine, when your paper says it's going to rain. John Whittaker, a Grinnell College anthropologist, said that trying to squelch "belief" is like stamping on a rubber spider: "It was never real. It simply can't be killed."

Atheism Is The Normal "Default Position" Of Rational People

Douglas E. Krueger, in his book "What is Atheism?" concludes that it is not necessary to know all about philosophy and religion in order to be an atheist because: (1) In the absence of any evidence of god's existence, the normal position of intelligent people is to be atheistic until some evidence shows up; (2) The concept of a "god" who knows everything and controls everything and reads our minds and sends us to hell or heaven is so inconsistent and incoherent that a rational person cannot accept it; (3) The existence of evil in the world (meaning bad and negative occurrences in the ordinary course of life) is evidence that a benevolent god is not running things or doesn't care; and (4) The existence of millions of non-Christians who have never heard of the Bible shows that a Christian god cannot be both all powerful, fair and benevolent.

St. Thomas Aquinas himself noted that the suffering of innocent people is what makes most people nonbelievers: "Nothing appears more to impugn divine providence in human affairs than the afflictions of the innocent ..." he said.

Then there is the fact that Christian Fundamentalists are simply no fun to have around because of their obsession with god and things "holy." They tend to be goody-goody people, queasy about sex. As Seinfeld said: "You don't ever really want to visualize your parents having sex. You don't want to think that your whole life began because somebody had a little too much wine with dinner, or your mother wore a very short skirt."

All Roads Lead To Atheism

George Smith wrote: "The theist is now on the defense; he can destroy atheism only by defending his belief in a god. If his defense fails, theism fails—and atheism emerges as the only rational alternative." Similarly, Flew said "We are left with the simple and economical though always defeasible presumption of ... atheism: the presumption that the universe is everything there is: and hence that everything which can be explained must be explained by reference to what is in and of the universe ... We therefore conclude, though as always subject to correction by further evidence and further argument, that the universe itself is ultimate; and, hence, that whatever science may from time to time hold to be the most fundamental laws of nature must, equally provisionally, be taken as the last words in any series of answers to questions as to why things are as they are."

Atheism Requires A Good Education

Atheism, then, is not merely opposition to religion: it is a way of thinking about everything rationally that inevitably results from considering these issues. "A man who will not reason about anything is no better than a vegetable," wrote Aristotle. Gould wrote "... we all know that atheists can live in the most firmly principled manner, while hypocrites can wrap themselves in any flag, including (most prominently) the banners of God and country." You can't recruit atheists like they recruit Democrats and Republicans, or AmWay distributors. There are not many acknowledged atheists because atheism is a philosophical view that requires a good education and the ability to think logically and rationally, *and it has no public role.* "Wanting to be an atheist does not make you one," said Napoleon Bonaparte.

In the 1920s and 1930s, in fact, agnosticism and atheism enjoyed a certain popularity among educated people in general, and books about atheism, such as Mencken's *Treatise on the*

Gods, were best sellers. The Scopes "Monkey Trial" in the 1920s, concerning the teaching of the Biblical creation story as truth, was good news for a long time. We still joke about it: "One day the zoo keeper noticed that the orangutan was reading two books, the Bible and Darwin's *Origin of Species,* and asked him why both books? "Well, said the orangutan, "I just wanted to know if I was my brother's keeper or my keeper's brother."

Religion Is Incompatible With 21st Century Knowledge

In the *Dictionary of the History of Ideas* (Scribners, 1973), a six-volume compilation of all ideas and scholarly thought, it is stated that "There is no longer any serious attempt to defend the truth of the cosmological claims in ... Biblical stories ... Huxley's arguments do come into conflict with conservative evangelism and his arguments about the plainly faulty, utter incoherence, and sometimes questionable morality of the miracle stories and stories of Jesus' actions." It is there stated that, "if there is such a clash, the scientific claims are clearly the claims to be preferred, for of all the rival ways of fixing belief, the scientific way of fixing belief is clearly the most reliable." Russell said "Practically all philosophers of any intellectual eminence are openly or secretly freethinkers." The article refers to Karl Popper, an eminent Austrian-British philosopher of the 20th century, in saying "that which cannot at least in principle be known by the method of science cannot be known."

There Are No Proofs of God's Existence

Ultimately, if there were any proofs of god's existence, atheism could not be seriously proposed. In a nutshell, scientific advancements of the 20th century have undermined the classic proofs of god, as follows:

- The Bible is a holy book written by god. There is no evidence of any kind for this theory, and thousands of scholars have explained satisfactorily how this folklore was in fact written. Books are not "magic" and the "creation story" is therefore intellectually false.

- The proposition that there must be a "first cause" to the world has been rejected by philosophers for the simple reason that there is neither a first cause for a god nor any evidence for a god existing apart from our universe. Some religionists continue to argue that god's existence can be proved by logical argument alone, such as variations of St. Anselm's argument used by the Catholic church, to the effect that god must exist as "that which nothing greater can be conceived." Mortimer Adler said … "this does not prove that the being we have thus conceived exists. It only proves that we can conceive of it." In other words, it is possible to construct an argument with words that leads only to the conclusion that god exits, but it is not possible to say that that argument relates to the world we actually live in without some kind of "leap of faith." Similarly, Simon Blackburn, professor of philosophy at the University of North Carolina, concluded that "we either have to ask what caused god himself or cut off the argument without conclusion."

- Scientists have shown that matter has existed since the Big Bang and that it can neither be annihilated nor exnihilated (meaning created out of nothing), so that matter must have existed before the Big Bang and will continue to exist even if our present universe ceases to exist.

- Scientists have also explained in technical terms how our universe developed and evolved, in such a way that there is no need for any "intelligent designer" existing outside of the universe.

- Based on scientific principles and research, there is no

evidence of anything "spiritual" in the universe (other than the electric impulses in our brains) and no evidence that human beings have a spiritual dimension or are able to send or receive any data by spiritual means. There is no evidence that the laws of physics have ever been suspended or superseded by anything spiritual or magic.

As Lily Tomlin once said, "We're all in this alone." On the other hand, Eugen Rosenstock-Huessy, who was a philosophy prof at Dartmouth College, said "He who believes in nothing still needs a girl who believes in him."

CHAPTER 3

WHERE ARE ALL THE ATHEISTS?

"I can very well do without God both in my life and in my painting, but I cannot, suffering as I am, do without something which is greater than I, which is my life, the power to create."
—Vincent van Gogh

Everybody's Got To Be Somewhere

Chances are that nobody you know is an atheist, or even that any of your friends and neighbors, etc., knows an atheist. "There are no atheists in my family, on my block, in this club," etc. There is an old joke about the man who got caught hiding in his lover's bedroom closet by her husband, who said "I have a logical excuse!" When the husband asked, "What excuse could you possibly have for being in *my wife's closet?*" the man replied: "Everybody's got to be *somewhere!*"

In an article published on November 20, 1999, Thomas Hargrove and Joseph Bernt reported that a study conducted by Scripps Howard News service and Ohio University has found that one out of every nine Americans—at least 24 million adults—does not belong to any organized religion. Only Roman Catholics exceed this group in numbers. The 11% who answer "none" when asked their religious preference tend to be male, young, urban and single. The article quoted the national spokesman for American Atheists, Inc., Ronald Barrier, as saying "One of the basic facts to being nonaligned with a religion is that you do not want restrictions imposed upon you … We [Atheists] are more open, more accepting."

The study found that one's "lifestyle" conditions the decision whether to attend regular worship services. Religious participation is low among the young, as 17% of young adults are church-free compared to 7% of people over 65. Single adults who have no children are more than twice as likely to be liberated from religion than are married people raising children. Only 8% of households with children are free of organized religion, compared to 18% of childless and single adults. Residents of large cities in the Northeast or on the Pacific Cost are less likely to attend church regularly than are people from small towns and rural regions in the Midwest or South. People unaligned in religion are also likely to be politically unaligned, with 16% of those who say they are "independent" of any party loyalties, compared to 9% of the self-professed "strong Democrats," and 6% of the "strong Republicans."

A recent article entitled "Confessions of a Lonely Atheist" in *The New York Times Magazine* said that only 3.2% of Americans said they didn't believe in god, as contrasted with 17.2% of the Dutch, 19.1% of the French, 16.8% of the Swedes, 20.3% of the Czechs, 19.7% of the Russians, 10.6% of the Japanese and 9.2% of the Canadians. *The majority of people in those countries said they do not believe in an afterlife.* (One conclusion that could logically be drawn is that American public education is below the European level: they are not taught "creationism").

Atheists in the Arts, Music, and Show Business

Tallulah Bankhead once said, to the censer preceding the bishop up the aisle at a Catholic service "Love your drag, honey, but did you know your purse is on fire?" In the last ten years, show business people (like Ellen De Generis) have been "coming out." Steve Allen, an entertainment maverick, said "No actual tyrant known to history has ever been guilty of one hundredth of the crimes, massacres, and other atrocities attributed to the Deity in the Bible." Frank Zappa said "Hey, let's get serious ... God knows what he's doin, ... He wrote this book here and the book says he made us all to be just like Him, so if we're dumb, then God is dumb (and maybe even a little ugly on the side)."

Woody Allen said "It's not that I'm afraid to die. I just don't want to be there when it happens." Archie Bunker said "Faith is when you believe something that nobody in his right mind would believe." Samuel Beckett said about god "The bastard! He doesn't exist!" Ingmar Bergman, the movie director, said "I hope I never get so old I get religious." Jane Curtin, the TV comic, joked (right after the Catholic Church said women cannot become priests because they do not resemble Christ) "Colonel Sanders just announced that he would not employ anyone who didn't resemble a chicken."

Thirties humorist Robert Benchley said "Everybody should believe in something; I believe I'll have another drink." Mike Reiss, the creator of "The Simpsons," wrote an item recently called "God is Dead, After Weather and Sports," in which he foretold that houses of worship would be forced to shut down when they lose their tax-exempt status: "Mosques became banks. Cathedrals were converted into multiplexes. Small churches became a chain of coffee shops called "St. Arbucks" ... In 2008 the Catholic Church had a massive going-out-of-business sale. "The Last Supper" now graces the lobby of Mitsubishi International in Osaka. The Sistine Chapel ceiling was moved intact to Trump's Vaticasino in Atlantic City. The Pope became just another celebrity, famous for being famous. He married Linda Evans."

Other non-believers in the entertainment field include: P.T. Barnum, Harvey Fierstein, Jodie Foster, Sir John Gielgud, Jean-Luc Godard, Katharine Hepburn, Teller (of Penn-and-), Stanley Kubrick, Ring Lardner Jr., Tom Lehrer, Randy Newman, Jack Nicholson, Roman Polanski, Ron Reagan Jr, Christopher Reeve, Mira Sorvino, Max von Sydow, P.G. Wodehouse, Dana Andrews, Ingmar Bergman, Marlon Brando, Dick Cavett, Charles Chaplin, Michael Crichton, Marlene Dietrich, Phyllis Diller, Frederico Fellini, W. C. Fields, Jane Fonda, Gypsy Rose Lee, Marcello Mastroianni, Zero Mostel, Sean Penn, Sally Jesse Raphael, Rod Steiger, Howard Stern, Uma Thurman, Peter Ustinov, Bruce Willis, Dana Andrews, John Barrymore, Bjork, Marlon Brando, Berthold Brecht, Charlie Chaplin, Bo Derek, Isadora Duncan, Hermione Gingold, Angelina Jolie, John Malkovich, Barry Manilow, Zero Mostel, Mike Nichols, Rudolf Nureyev, Sean Penn, James Randi, Christopher Reeve, Sally Jesse Raphael, Rimsky-Korsakov, Pete Seeger, Howard Stern, James Taylor, James Thurber, Bruce Willis, Larry King, and Norman Lear.

Dana Andrews, a very popular 1940-50s movie actor, said: "People need something to sustain them in times of crisis or at times of loss. But more and more today it seems like the old answers just don't fit ... Sometimes we want to stop the world, and get off. Once I felt like that and then I found a life philosophy called humanism. It gave me the strength to get over the bad times ... Humanists believe in having faith in humanity, in human beings helping one another."

Hollywood still has its famous believers, of course, like Shirley MacLaine and Richard Gere, who believe in spiritualism, and John Travolta and Tom Cruise, who are followers of O. Ron Hubbard's "Scientology" racket-cult based on something unscientific called "engrams" in the human body (which no medical doctor or scientist has ever found) and on Hubbard's con that the "soul" can be "cleaned up" by "processing" it. If you lack a good education, or are just not very smart, all ideas seem equal, so you just close your eyes and pick one.

When it comes to music, atheists abound. Beethoven said, after being given his last rites, "Applaud, friends, the comedy is over." Sarah Bernhardt said "Me pray? Never! I'm an atheist." Others are Berlioz, Brahms, Debussy, Mahler, Mozart, Schubert, Schumann, Richard Strauss, Tchaikowsky, Saint-Saens, Wagner, Bizet, Boulez, Britten, Debussy, Grieg, Haydn, Paganini, Rampal, Rimsky-Korsakov, and Verdi. In popular music, there is Billy Joel, Tom Lehrer, Barry Manilow, Jim Morrison, Randy Newman, Pete Seeger and Woody Allen (who plays jazz clarinet).

Atheists in Foxholes

During wartime, political and military leaders are fond of saying "There are no atheists in foxholes." What that really means is there are a lot of atheists in foxholes who then ask themselves: what have I got to lose *now*? That is similar to the argument for god that Pascal used: although there seems to be no evidence of god, it doesn't cost me anything to pray, making it a good gamble, something like after-life insurance.

Religious people make good soldiers because they think the worst that can happen is that they spend more time in heaven and less time on earth. If the enemy is referred to as "godless," religionists are more likely to take a personal interest in killing them. The foxholes in Iran and Iraq, of course, were filled with religious soldiers eager to die for their religion, so they would be "martyrs" who enjoy a special status in heaven. *Iran and Iraq are probably the best examples of the religious approach to problem-solving today: kill the enemy and then die yourself to please god.* A recent newspaper article featured an

Afghan revolutionary who had killed over 100 "enemies of God" as a matter of deep religious conviction. Historically, Christians, too, love to go war against infidels, as in the case of the Medieval Crusades to the Holy Land.

In World War II, the Korean War and the Vietnam War, large numbers of disillusioned foot solders ignored the outdoor religious services, preferring to sleep or, in Vietnam, drink a beer or smoke a joint if they could, or listen to rock music. Death in combat is seen by thousands of soldiers as a waste of human life—their own, especially. Nobody believed that the Viet Cong were about to invade Geneva, Illinois. "War is God's way of teaching us geography," said Paul Rodriguez, trying to look on the bright side. The idea that everything in life is pre-determined by god is very popular with generals and Hollywood producers. Each bullet coming your way is predetermined either (a) to kill you, or (b) to miss you. In war movies they say: "Either it's got my number on it or it hasn't! There's nothing I can do about it, so let's give it to 'em, boys! Fix bayonets!"

According to Prof. Blackburn, the proper reply is: "… whether a bullet has your number on it or not may very well depend on whether you choose to wear a helmet." So much for Fate! "God is always on the side of the big battalions," said Napoleon, Voltaire, Frederick the Great, Tacitus, and probably hundreds of others. There seems to be no evidence, on the other hand, that atheists are not good soldiers. In battle, of course, there are limits to what a chaplain can do, even if he is very brave. On the other hand, they have nothing but their temporary, brief, wicked, earthly lives to lose, crawling from foxhole to foxhole. "Your mother sent you this cake! What religion are you, soldier?"

"Keep your head down, Chaplain! Well, my mother was Jewish and my father was a Christian Scientist." Craaaaaaack!

"Wow that was a close one! We don't have any of those, soldier! How about the Lord's Prayer?" Kerpooooowwwwwoow!

"Keep your head down, Chaplain, you're *drawing fire!* What are you doing? Keep the cake! There's no room in here! Chaplain? Chaplain? Medic! Medic!" (Let's face it: an atheist *knows* that he is risking *everything—forever!* Now who is the bravest?

Atheist Political Leaders

Certainly in today's political atmosphere an atheist or agnostic could not get nominated for dog-catcher, unlike Adlai Stevenson, who was the Democratic candidate against Eisenhower. It seems hard to believe now, but Adlai's nonreligious beliefs were not even an issue in the 1956 campaign.

The following Presidents were atheists or agnostics: Washington, Madison, Jefferson, John Adams, John Quincy Adams, Millard Fillmore, Lincoln and Harding. (It appears that there were no Christian Fundamentalists lobbying against those Presidents.) Other famous and admired politicians in that category are Paul Revere, John Hancock, Aaron Burr, John Calhoun, and William Pitt Jr. More recent American figures include Robert La Follette, Sen. Alan Cranston and Elliot Richardson. For what it's worth, other famous political figures include Simon Bolivar, Napoleon, Willy Brandt, Julius Caesar, Neville Chamberlain, Clemenceau, Hugh Gaitskell, Neil Kinnock, Harold Laski, Marcus Aurelius, Nehru, Raymond Poincare, Cecil Rhodes, Leland Stanford, Talleyrand and Queen Victoria.

Atheists Among The Poor And Disadvantaged

In his best-selling book, *Cultural Literacy*, E.D Hirsch, Jr. wrote that children not only learn about our world through general principles, as Dewey said, but that there is simply no substitute for "piling up knowledge." If we don't do that, Hirsch wrote, children from disadvantaged families cannot succeed in our present, complex society. One reason why high school and college grads today do not have the kind and range of knowledge people had 50 years ago, said Hirsch, is that much of the knowledge we need to think complex thoughts are taught by educated parents to their children as they grow up, while children of less educated parents do not have that kind of parental education. That alone is a big advantage for white, Protestant Americans in school and in the workplace. He wrote: "… in the United States, only two-thirds of our citizens are literate, and even among those the average level is too low …" Although Hirsch was not concerned with the ability to understand the concept of atheism, the implication of his research is obvious: *only two thirds of our population (and probably less) is capable of being rational.*

Even worse is the inability of millions of Americans to learn how to think, or to even understand the issues involved in agnosticism, atheism, science and rational thinking, not to mention political theory. That may mean, at the crudest level, that American politics at all levels, from the school board to Congress, is doomed to remain confused and irrational. *If the point of Hirsch's book is even partly sound, atheism is not an idea that millions of Americans can even understand.* It is like a lot of other things that they can't understand, such as physics, geology, biology, history, architecture, electronics, computers, Latin, etc. If that is correct, there are few atheists among manual laborers, messengers, soldiers, short-order cooks, retail sales people, warehouse handlers, etc., and maybe not even in the police forces.

Cultural literacy is "the network of information that all competent readers possess." Hirsch wrote: "Illiterate and semi-literate Americans are condemned not only to poverty, but also to the powerlessness of incomprehension. Knowing that they do not understand the issues, and feeling prey to manipulative oversimplification, they do not trust the system of which they are supposed to be the masters." The inference is that one-third of our population will remain religious because religion—

although imaginary—is easy to understand as a concept and as a ritual.

Atheists Behind Bars

It seems to be a truism that very religious people are more lax about complying with secular laws than non-believers. For example, religious people who violate tax or traffic laws, etc., often argue that they put "God's law" first since it is "more important" or "higher." In the case of Catholics, that may be the availability of confession, which gives their conscience a little cushion that Methodists or atheists don't have. A comedian named Emo Philips saw humor in it: "When I was a kid, I used to pray every night for a new bicycle. Then I realized that the system doesn't work that way, and I figured it out. So I stole one, and asked God to forgive me."

Fundamentalists think that the main point of god is *not* to forgive them. Does that mean that more bikes are stolen by Catholics? If well-known novels and biographies are any guide, Catholics traditionally deal with prostitutes more than Methodists or Lutherans, for example, and gamble more. To a Catholic, such violations may be hard to take seriously because they are *officially* only "minor sins." By the same token, an atheist is more apt to follow all secular laws very carefully, including speeding laws, drinking laws, drug laws, hunting and fishing laws, etc., as a matter of conscience, or even honor, because there are no other laws to follow.

Logically, with only secular laws to follow, atheists would tend to be more observant than religionists who must follow "higher laws," etc. Breaking speed limits is likely to seem more trivial to a religionist than to an atheist, who is conscious of the importance of reciprocity and the civil law precisely because nobody upstairs is looking. Also, there have been recent news articles about Protestant ministers who refuse to pay income taxes because "God is above secular law." For example, the

Indianapolis Baptist Temple refused to pay taxes in protest of "liberal" government spending. Their leaders also threatened to refuse fire inspections and use ZIP codes, on the ground that only god's laws apply. Similarly, the Rev. Daniel Little, whose flock is located near Binghamton, NY, published a newspaper ad asking for donations to defeat Bill Clinton in 1992 because he supported policies that are against God's laws. When the church's tax exemption was then revoked for political activity, Rev. Little's response was typical of the Fundamentalists: "Principle takes precedence over silly laws."

Flew cites a study showing that young people with a religious education are more likely to become "juvenile delinquents" than those raised without a religion. That may be due to the fact that parents who choose to raise children without religion pay closer attention to their moral and ethical development. He points out, for example, that the evidence we have generally shows high positive correlation between Roman Catholicism and delinquency, as well as some signs of a negative correlation with "nonconformity."

Flew says that shows, first, that religious denomination may be relevant to delinquency, and second, "that it is impudent for Roman Catholics to put forward, as one reason for getting still more tax money for their parochial schools, claims that what is there provided constitutes a bulwark against delinquency." (Flew cites *Religious Behaviour*, by Michael Argyle).

According to Richard Posner: "Countless studies show higher rates of religious affiliation among criminals and juvenile delinquents than among the rest of the population. In addition, the three countries with the highest religious attendance in the world (U.S.A., Ireland, and South Africa) have an extremely high violence rate, where the three countries with lowest religious attendance (Denmark, Sweden, and Japan) have an unusually low rate of violence." That is to say, religion makes us unreasonable and passionate at the same time. In any case, it certainly cannot be said that religion in general promotes virtue and obedience to the law and reduces our prison population, which is comprised almost solely of people raised with a religion.

Atheists on the Gridiron

Don't look for atheists on the gridiron. It is a common sight to see the coaches of both teams leading the guys in prayer before game time. One wonders, of course, why they do that, when obviously, only one side can win. Worse, it implies that god in fact favors the team that won. "I give the same half-time speech over and over," said Chuck Mills. "It works best when my players are better than the other coach's players." Jeff Stilson said "I don't like the interview after the game, because the winning players always give credit to God while the losing players blame themselves. Just once I'd like to hear a player say, Yeah, we were in the game until Jesus made me fumble!"

Which brings us to more individual sports and pastimes, which is where the atheists are: mountain climbers, scuba divers, sports that don't require cooperation with others. For example, long distance runners, cross country skiers, bow and arrow marksmen, and certain esoteric sports like surfing, hang gliding, parachuting, bobsledding, building and flying homemade airplanes, etc., things that require some technical mastery or tremendous concentration. The guy that shows you the best mountain climbing boot on sale anywhere is not unlikely to be an atheist; atheists care a lot about the *self*, including equipment, gear, gadgets, and the great outdoors. Few of them go to church because Sunday is when they do their favorite thing.

Atheist Techies and Inventors

Late 20th century technology, let's face it, attracted nonbelievers like honey does bees, including Edison, Bell, Steinmetz, Burbank, and now Bill Gates. Edison said "So far as religion of the day is concerned, it is a damned fake ... Religion is all bunk." *What he invented was real.* While some people who are clever with their hands like to say that god inspires them and guides their hands, most of them know that skills are developed by perseverance and practice. "How do you get to Carnegie Hall?" is a common question, and the answer usually is "Practice, practice and practice," rather than "pray, pray and pray."

Starting with the hi-fi tweeter and woofer craze, atheists gravitated to high-tech gear. They liked the new, big tennis rackets, the running shoes, the new short, plastic skis, the snowboards, the 21-speed racing bikes, the endless gadgets for computers. They like lightweight but warm camping equipment like tents, sleeping bags, headlamps, etc. They like kayaks and gliders (but not snowmobiles and water scooters that pollute, *maybe because, for atheists, ethics takes the place of worship).*

Let's face it, a vast proportion of people we like to call nerds grow up to be atheists because they do not give a damn what other people think. The reason most parents become alarmed when their kid turns into a nerd is not just that he or she is smart, but that they don't want to go to church any more because there are more interesting things to do on Sunday morning. Guys who build their own TV reception disks and astronomic telescopes are very likely to be atheists, as a matter of observation, common sense, and inductive reasoning. Many inventors, too, and artists of all kinds, have always been religious skeptics. A musician or cabinet maker or other artist is more likely to credit his own genius and perseverance than credit God. "He was a wise man who invented God," said Plato.

Atheist Writers

Here are the atheists, folks! Shakespeare was not religious and never mentioned the Christian God or saints, etc., in his works. His plays include lines like the following: "In religion, what damned error but some sober brow will bless it … .?" *(Merchant of Venice)*. "Thrust your head into the public street, to gaze on Christian fools …" *(Merchant of Venice)*. "Methinks sometimes I have no more wit than a Christian" *(Twelfth Night)*. "His worst fault is, he's given to prayer …" *(The Merry Wives of Windsor)*. Henry Fielding wrote: "No man has ever sat down calmly unbiased to reason out his religion and not ended by rejecting it." Samuel Butler wrote: Christ was crucified once, and for a few hours. Think of the thousands he has been crucifying in a quiet way ever since." Robert Burns wrote: "God knows I'm no the thing I should be / Nor am I even the thing I could be / But, twenty times, I rather would be An atheist clean / Than under gospel colors hid be, Just for the screen."

Here are some more quotations from Emerson, one of America's leading men of letters: "Other world? There is no other world! Here or nowhere is the whole fact;" "A foolish consistency is the hobgoblin of little minds, adored by little statesmen and philosophers and divines;" "When Nature has work to be done, she creates a genius to do it;" "The cure for theology is mother-wit;" and "As men's prayers are a disease of the will, so are their creeds a disease of the intellect." Unfortunately, schoolboards filter out the real Emerson.

Stendhal said: "All religions are founded on the fear of the many and the cleverness of the few." Joseph Conrad wrote: "The ethical view of the universe involves us in so many cruel and absurd contradictions that I have come to suspect that the aim of creation cannot be ethical at all." Jack Kerouac said "I'm a Catholic and I can't commit suicide, but I plan to drink myself to death." (In the Catholic religion, sin is more of a technicality.) Jules Feiffer said "Christ died for our sins. Dare we make his martyrdom meaningless by not committing them?" Atheist poets also include Bryant, Burns, Butler, Byron, e e cummings, Emily Dickinson, Lawrence Ferlinghetti, John

Keats, Amy Lowell, Robert Lowell, Frank O'Hara, May Sarton, Algernon Swinburne, Tennyson, William Carlos Willims and Wordsworth.

It is easy to see why Christian Fundies want to change reality by censoring library books.

Other atheist and agnostic authors include: Horatio Alger, Arnold Bennett, Bocaccio, Van Wyck Brooks, Anthony Burgess, James B. Cabell, Albert Camus, Thomas Carlyle, Anton Chekhov, Samuel Clemens, Samuel Taylor Coleridge, Joseph Conrad, Norman Cousins, Quentin Crisp, Daniel Defoe, Charles Dickens, Theodore Dreiser, Alexandre Dumas, George Eliot, James T. Farrell, William Faulkner, Henry Fielding, Scott Fitzgerald, John Fowles, Anatole France, John Galsworthy, Johann von Goethe, Oliver Goldsmith, Lorraine Hansberry, Bret Harte, Nathaniel Hawthorne, Lillian Hellman, Nat Hentoff, Oliver Wendell Holmes Jr., A. E. Housman, Victor Hugo, Aldous Huxley, Henrik Ibsen, James Joyce, Franz Kafka, Ken Kesey, Arthur Koestler, Charles Lamb, Ring Lardner Jr., Sinclair Lewis, Jack London, Longfellow, Archibald MacLeish, Andre Malraux, Thomas Mann, John P. Marquand, Somerset Maugham, Guy de Maupassant, Mary McCarthy, Herman Melville, James Michener, Edna St. Vincent Millay, Arthur Miller, Moliere, Iris Murdoch, Sean O'Casey, Eugene O'Neill, Camille Paglia, Harold Pinter, Edgar Allan Poe, Marcel Proust, Edmond Rostand, Rousseau, Salman Rushdie, Georges Sand, Carl Sandburg, Rod Serling, G. B. Shaw, Percy B. Shelley, Terry Southern, Lincoln Steffens, John Steinbeck, Stendhal, Robert L. Stevenson, Tom Stoppard, William Styron, Henry Thoreau, Lionel Trilling, Carl Van Doren, Mario Vargas Llosa, Gore Vidal, Voltaire, Kurt Vonnegut, Alice Walker, Horace Walpole, Walt Whitman, William Carlos Williams, Sloan Wilson, P.G. Wode-house, Virginia Woolf and Emile Zola. Playwrights include Beckett, Brecht, Fierstein, Marlow, Pinter, Pirandello, Shaw, Stoppard, Strindberg, Voltaire, Rousseau, and Isaac Azimov.

Atheists in Las Vegas

You won't find many atheists in Las Vegas or Atlantic City, or standing in line for a lottery ticket, because atheists tend to be logical, analytical thinkers. Most atheists understand things like the law of averages and probability theories. It is a mathematical fact that the more you play the more the odds build against you, except for an infinitesimally small percentage of lottery addicts who actually hit the big one.

Atheists In The Library

They may well be in your public library, just down the block. At least one of them is an atheist or agnostic, although they won't admit that in the South. According to the American Library Association, there are approximately 10,000 librarians in the U.S. They said they do not know how many of these are atheists. The point is, no matter how many librarians there are, the number of atheists in libraries is not large enough to do any real damage to American civilization. Atheists like books, particularly reference books and encyclopedias, and history and science books.

Atheists In The Courtroom

Yes, folks, there are atheists in the courtroom. Polls show that the average American does not like lawyers. Christians don't like lawyers because they seem to be without principles: without breaking stride, they can represent a communist one day and a fascist the next; a murderer one day and a victim's husband the next. Christians think in terms of right and wrong, not guilt and innocence. Lawyers are perceived as prostitutes, available to do anything for money. That, of course, is only partly true. Whatever they do, however, they do within the framework of the U.S. Constitution, which, for many of them, is their real religion. The same kind of lawyers win cases upholding the right to own guns, and the right to hold far-out liberal views. YES! There are atheists at the Bar! And most of them don't mind a dry martini once in a while.

Atheists Among The Shrinks

The odds are pretty good that your shrink is an atheist because he/she has studied how the brain works. They know what emotions and feelings are, and how they differ from knowledge that is stored in the brain. Nothing that a psychiatrist learns in graduate school deals with miracles, talking to god, or hearing holy voices in their heads. There are a few "orthodox shrinks" and some "Christian shrinks" who cater to religious patients. Probably, there are very few Christian Fundamentalist shrinks for the simple reason that psychiatry is a body of scientific knowledge and as a treatment is incompatible with bedrock beliefs of the Bible. What can a shrink say to a hard-shell Baptist who thinks the Devil is on his back or in his basement, or that the world is about to end?

Journalists

Atheists like it here, too, because, usually, journalism is an individual occupation, not a group thing. Andy Rooney said "No, of course I don't [believe in god] and anyone who tells you that there is a god who makes his or her presence known to him or her is hallucinating or not telling the truth." Other journalists include Russell Baker, John Chancellor, Linda Ellerbee, Molly Ivins, Wendy Kaminer, Larry King, Max Lerner, Walter Lippmann, Harold Ross, Arthur Ochs Sulzberger and Marilyn Vos Savant.

While young journalists often learn their trade by helping a more experienced person, as is the case with almost every other occupation, sooner or later they find themselves on their own, often for extended periods of time and often in unfamiliar surroundings. Ambrose Bierce, who is well known for dozens of quotable observations of the human condition, was a newspaper reporter for the Hearst newspapers in the late 19th century. He was a battle-scarred combat veteran of the Civil War himself. He was also, by any measurement, one of the funniest men alive, as well as one of America's foremost literary stylists. He became well-known for covering the Mexican revolution in the early 1900s, including travels with Pancho Villa, where he was last seen alive. Bierce wrote a funny book called *The Devil's Dictionary*, which was very popular among educated, nonreligious people in the early 20th century.

Atheists In Our Universities And Labs

If you are looking for atheists in any great numbers, here is where they are, folks! A Christian Fundamentalist was quoted as saying, in a 1999 speech somewhere in Florida, that there are 10,000 "communists" in American universities. Since no such records are kept, and university catalogs have no courses on communism (outside of history and government courses), the man was obviously confused. Since there are no courses labeled "atheism" in university catalogs, he probably meant our teachers of philosophy. A recent *New York Times* article about philosophy teachers said that there are roughly 9,000 philosophy Ph.D's teaching in the U.S. By that standard, philosophy itself is subversive! All those courses teach "how the world works" *without mentioning god*. In fact, many people who teach such subjects are Christians, although not Fundamentalists.

There are, of course, atheists in all occupations, for the simple reason that most people choose their occupation long before they have experience enough to become atheists. Avram Chomsky, a well-known linguistics professor at M.I.T., lamented that "... the figures are shocking. Three-quarters of the American population literally believe in religious miracles. The numbers who believe in the devil, in resurrection, in God doing this and that—it's astonishing. These numbers aren't duplicated anywhere else in the industrial world. You'd have to maybe go to mosques in Iran or do a poll among old ladies in Sicily to get numbers like this."

Madame Curie, the discoverer of radium, wrote: "Here lies an atheist; All dried up, And no place to go." Nobody is surprised that winners of the Nobel Prize in science include more atheists than others, and that leading intellectuals and thinkers generally are often agnostics or atheists, so there is no point in listing those names here. The reference book *Who's Who in Hell* in your public library shows very strikingly that the majority of prize-winning scientists have been and are atheists or agnostics, which strongly suggests that the smartest people in the world do not believe in god or religion.

Where Do Atheists Look For Jobs?

Are you a non-believer personality type? *You find atheists—and jobs atheists like—by a process of induction, like scientists do when they are looking for some kind of elusive pulsating star or an endangered species: you simply make a list of where most people are, and then—one by one—eliminate atheists from those lists. There may well be "an atheist personality."* The sociology pioneer Gordon Allport said that we all require a unifying philosophy of life or a system of values that will direct and give meaning to our lives. He says there are six personality types: theoretical (searching for truth); the economic (practical); the esthetic (artistic); the social (gregarious); the political (interested in power and influence); and the religious (having mystical beliefs.) Some of us have several of these traits. *Clearly, atheists are more likely to be theoretical and practical, while religionists are more likely to be social or political.*

Another well-known theory is based on the "tough-minded" vs. "tender-minded" classification. The tough-minded are emotionally neutral, independent, hard and realistic, holding back feelings, not wishful thinkers, self-sufficient, and not anxious. The tender-minded are demanding, impatient, dependent, immature, gentle, sentimental, fastidious, imaginative, anxious, and gregarious. Both classifications are "normal" from a mental health standpoint: each of us is one or the other. Most people are tender-minded (meaning flexible or malleable), while atheists are likely to be tough-minded (inflexible or resistant).

In other words, atheists tend to be people who look at the world intellectually and practically, relying on their own judgment, and religionists are people who look at the world emotionally and idealistically, relying on the judgment of people around them. This theory is somewhat similar to the categories for introverts (passive, careful, thoughtful, peaceful, controlled, reliable, even-tempered and calm) and extraverts (sociable, outgoing, talkative, responsive, easy-going, lively, carefree and willing leaders). It seems more than likely that atheists are likely to be introverts and religious people are extraverts, because atheists are private and thoughtful and religionists are public and social. A sociologist named Sternberg wrote in 1985 that we all function intellectually in three aspects: analytical (good at taking tests); experiential (thinking creatively); and contextual, meaning "street-smarts," getting along with and manipulating people. It would appear obvious that atheists would be good at taking tests, while religionists would be good at street smarts, meaning getting along with (and manipulating) other people.

In the 1950s, sociologist David Riesman divided people into "inner-directed' and "other-directed," meaning that some people go along with the crowd and some are more independent. In his textbook, *Introduction to Personality*, E. Jerry Phares, a well-known sociologist, agrees that different personality types exist and that they have distinctive characteristics. In his book, these categories are expressed as "externally controlled" vs. "internally controlled" in the context of reacting to the outside world. Logically, most religionists are more affected by events outside their own personal lives, while atheists are most affected by their own thinking, regardless of external influences. *For example, a religionist typically would believe that much of what happens to him is probably a matter of luck, or controlled by god, etc., being a small part of a much bigger picture. On the contrary, an atheist often believes that much of what happens to him is a matter of his own conduct and thinking, and within his control.*

Phares says "Perhaps the most fundamental difference between Internals and Externals lies in the way they seek knowledge about their environment." In tune with Internals' beliefs that they are masters of their own fate, they seem to seek out actively the information that will permit them to live the way they prefer. While Phares' sociological studies had nothing to do with atheism, the values inherent in the studies clearly show that atheists are probably nonconformists guided mostly by "internal" factors. "By definition, internals attribute to themselves the responsibility for the outcomes of their own behavior. Externals, in contrast, attribute that responsibility elsewhere." For example, Phares cites studies concerning responsibility for automobile accidents: externals tended not to blame the drivers themselves (probably considering that god runs the world and accidents occur all the time) while internals believed in personal responsibility for whatever happens. In general, Phares showed that internals are more likely to seek information, be resistant to social influence and attribute responsibility to themselves and others. Internals generally do better in learning new subjects, *without teacher input*, especially where standardized tests are used.

Individuals who, for whatever reasons, enjoy little access to power, social mobility, opportunity or material advantages would be predisposed toward an external belief system. Their cumulative experience would teach them that their own efforts have little to do with their achievement in society. Scientists, college instructors, political independents, physicians, engineers and inventors, then, would typically be internals, while social workers, salesmen, business executives, soldiers and religionists would typically be externals. *In other words, people who see life as something much bigger than they are tend to conform to the views of others, while those who see life as a personal venture, with a lot of personal responsibility on a continuous basis, tend to be Internals.* By definition, a religionist thinks that god controls his/her life and an atheist thinks he/she is in control personally.

It may well be that "inner directed" or internally oriented people are better citizens precisely because they do not need social pressures to act morally and honestly. By definition, they carry their moral compasses in their own heads. If those categories mean anything at all, if minor crime is rampant in any area or sector or generation, it will be spread more easily among externally directed people than among internally oriented people who by definition are less easily tempted or corrupted.

Certainly, high school rapists are the externally influenced jocks and not the internally oriented geeks and nerds, musicians and honor students.

Matching Atheist Personality To Occupation

Books on job-hunting also are based on "personality types." One such book is *"Real People, Real Jobs,"* by a man named Holland, who devised the "Holland Hexagon," showing six major categories of jobs based on personality, background and goals, etc. Each point in his hexagon represents a general "personality theme," as follows: realistic, investigative, artistic, social, enterprising and conventional. Under the Holland scheme, everybody has three of such themes, including one dominant one and two minor ones. While atheists could be in all six categories, logic dictates that they tend to be in the realistic, investigative and artistic categories. For example, realistic includes interests like mechanics, outdoors, plants, animals, and tangible results. Investigative includes themes like problem-solving, analytical skills, mathematics, generating ideas, working alone, research, intellectual, science, teaching, medicine, "high tech," etc. Artistic means creative, idealistic, independent, writing, painting and acting. Those three themes are next to each other on the hexagon.

Holland's classification is probably right, however, in that most businessmen, politicians, salesmen and policemen are not atheists.

Another such book is *Do What you Are* by Paul D. Tieger and Barbara Barron-Tieger (Little, Brown and Co., 1995), which is also based upon an alleged scientific "personality type" analysis, of which there are four, each covered by one of the following personality determinants: extraversion vs. introversion; sensing vs. intuition; thinking vs. feeling; and judging vs. perceiving—making 16 possible types of people if you make all possible combinations. For example, the introverted, sensing, thinking and perceiving (ISTP) category includes approximately 6% of Americans. "ISTP's are straightforward, honest and pragmatic people who prefer action to conversation. They are unpretentious and often have a good understanding of the way things work. Because they are analytical, ISTPs are most interested in the impersonal and underlying principles of things. ISTPs have an innate understanding of how mechanical things work and are usually skilled at using tools and working with their hands. They tend to make logical and private decisions, stating things clearly and directly, just as they see them. Curious and observant, ISTPs tend to be convinced only by hard, reliable facts. They have a great respect for facts and can be veritable storehouses of information on the things they know well and understand. Because they are realists, they are able to capitalize well on available resources, which makes them practical, with a good sense of timing. Quiet and reserved,

ISTPs tend to appear cool and aloof and are inclined to wary shyness, except when with good friends. They are self-leading, egalitarian, and fair. They tend to operate on impulse, so they are quite adaptable and responsive to immediate challenges and problems. Because they thrive on excitement and action, they usually like the outdoors and sports." (This category describes an introverted atheist.) By contrast, an extroverted atheist (in the extraverted, sensing, thinking and perceiving category, i.e., the same thing as above except for extraversion), would have slightly different traits. While any skeptic can become an agnostic, a good education plus the ability to think rationally is required to be an atheist. Atheists are created by education, not born that way.

COMPETITION IN THE GARDEN OF EDEN.

CHAPTER 4

MORALITY

"The defence of morals is the battle-cry which best rallies stupidity against change."
—Alfred N. Whitehead

Morality, like weather, is a question of geography and time. Steve Martin recently wrote an article called "Morality Through the Centuries," as follows: "The history of thought not only deals with philosophy but ethics and morality as well. I offer the advanced student of moral history the following summary:

Roman era: anything goes
Medieval era: nothing goes
Renaissance: anything goes
Seventeenth century Spain: nothing goes
Eighteenth century France: anything goes
Nineteenth century England: nothing goes
1920s America: anything goes
1950s America: nothing goes
1990s America: anything goes

Even as rhythmic as these statistics are," said Steve, "it is impossible to predict the moral tenor of even the next few years, because of the Elvis factor. The Elvis factor is the tendency of an era with one consistent and rigid moral philosophy to be upset and radically altered by a simple, uneducated hillbilly with a new idea."

Morality Has Nothing To Do With Religion

Manners change and morals change; men remain," said John Galsworthy. Professor Kurtz wrote: *"Morality can be made a part of religion but is not a necessary part of it ..."* According to *Encyclopedia Americana,* morality is nothing more than the standard of "good" and "bad," and "fairness" adopted by any civilization. "The problem is how to construct a world in which immoral people can do the least harm; not how to enable moral people to do the most good," said Milton Friedman. Einstein said "A man's ethical behavior should be based effectually on sympathy, education, and social ties; no religious basis is necessary. Man would indeed be in a poor way if he had to be restrained by fear of punishment and hope of regard after death ..."

Christianity, like almost every well-developed culture, has a "golden rule" of reciprocity that applies to human relationships in general, covering morality as well as general ethics. The Talmud says the same thing: "What is hateful to you, do not to your fellow; that is the whole Law; all the rest is interpretation." The Hindu Mahabharata states: "This is the sum of all true righteousness: deal with others as thou wouldst thyself be dealt by. Do nothing to thy neighbor which thou would not have him do to thee hereafter." Humans understood and respected moral rules long before America's Christian Fundamentalists existed. It would appear that most advanced societies agree on some kind of bedrock ethical and moral rules even though they disagree violently on matters of religion. It also says "When man appears before the Throne of Judgment, the first question he will be asked is not 'Have you believed in God' or 'Have you prayed and observed the ritual?'—but 'Have you dealt honorably with your fellow man?' " It is an example of religion endorsing morality. Plato, Aristotle and Confucius also recognized that before Christianity existed.

Milton Friedman said "The problem is how to construct a world in which immoral people can do the least harm; not how to enable moral people to do the most good." There are always bad guys who are not bound by the rule. In fact, religion is only a minor part of morality. Pierre Joseph Proudhon, a nineteenth century French liberal thinker, said *Man is destined to live without religion, but the moral law is eternal and absolute. Who would dare today to attack morality?*

Thus, although morality is relative, religion is absolute. Sinbad (the comedian, not the sailor) said "You're never too fat or too thin; it's all in the people you're hanging with. If you're big, stick with people bigger than you, and they'll call you Slim. If you're skinny, go with people who are scrawny, and feel bulked up." If you hang out with Christian Fundamentalists, they will look down on you; if you hang out with prostitutes, they will look up to you.

Ayn Rand, one of the few famous atheists of the 20th century, wrote: "What is morality, or ethics? It is a code of values to guide man's choices and actions—the choices and actions that determine the purpose and the course of his life." She also wrote: "… if devotion to truth is the hallmark of morality, then there is no greater, nobler, more heroic form of devotion than the act of a man who assumes the responsibility of thinking."

Whitehead warned: "As our society is now constituted, a literal adherence to the moral precepts scattered throughout the Gospels would mean sudden death." *The Bible does not provide a moral system.* It is solely a matter of what god wants us to do to get to heaven. You can find Biblical support for conduct civilized people no longer consider appropriate or decent.

There is only the Ten Commandments of the Hebrews, which although generally ethical, are not a code of earthly conduct in a complex society (being intended only to please a wrathful god in a primitive society). "Love thy neighbor as thyself" is not a practical moral system for the 20th century, but only an over-generalized, idealized goal for elderly people waiting in line for heaven. "Loving your neighbor as much as yourself is practically bloody impossible ... you might as well have a command-ment that states: thou shalt fly," said John Cleese, the Monty Python tall guy.

A former governor of Texas who lied about a famous SMU football scandal defended himself as follows: "Well, there never was a Bible in the room" (meaning that you can't violate morals and ethics if you are not holding or looking at a Bible, or one is within reach, as if the presence of a Bible itself is "magic," whether you are reading it or not).

Wendy Kaminer said "... faith in immaterial realities is popularly considered essential to individual morality ... There is a double standard here, in that in the real world the normal, everyday things people do are condemned." Wilde said "The books that the world call immoral are the books that show the world its own shame." Obviously, our culture is really confused about what morality is.

Religion Is Often Immoral

Krueger explained that the Bible is a very primitive, crude and inadequate source for moral principles; that it recommends all kinds of actions that are in fact immoral, including racism, sexism, blindly obeying political leaders, genocide, lying and murder. He points out the obvious fact that, if you have to fol-low some parts of the Bible that are good and ignore other parts because they are evil, then the Bible is not authoritative for any-thing. "The foundation of morality is to have done, once and for all, with lying," said Thomas H. Huxley. H. G. Wells said:

"Moral indignation is jealousy with a halo."

Kant said "There is only a single categorical imperative and it is this: Act only on that maxim through which you can at the same time will that it should become a universal law!" To Kant, acting morally was an *imperative*, meaning that, if a system of morality could be devised by reason alone, we, being rational people (Kant was an optimist), should follow it because human beings are moral, rational creatures.

Morality Is Used As A Tool To Support Religion

In America, morality is often used as a stick by religion-ists to beat their enemies. Nietzsche agreed that morality is often used as a tool by religion to influence human activities: "Morality is the herd-instinct in the individual." He also said "Morality is the best of all devices for leading mankind by the nose." He explained that "In Christianity neither morality nor religion come into contact with reality at any point." In the same vein, Wilde said "I never came across anyone in whom the moral sense was dominant who was not heartless, cruel, vindictive, log-stupid, and entirely lacking in the smallest sense of humanity."

According to scholars, morality is a real, social concern, not an individual's concern about his soul. In recent times, morality, then, separated from religion, focuses on what is "right" and "good" either legally or ethically. Since the Enlightenment, philosophers have told us that it is human nature to love oneself and one's family first, and to cherish or value those in one's circle that includes friends, employers and employees, teammates, etc., in that order. It only makes sense to love everybody all the time if you are standing in line for admission to heaven, where that kind of standard would actu-ally work. *There is no such thing as a religious morality that can be effective in the real world, and the truth of that statement is that even the most devout Christians, Muslims and Jews do not*

even try to practice it. Its various commands are inconsistent.
For example, that we should not resist evil, that slavery is an
okay thing, that gentiles are less human, that murder can be
justified on practical grounds, that all government authorities
should be obeyed, that women may properly be oppressed, that
children of Israel's enemies may be killed, that lying may be justified, etc. "After all, it is setting a high value upon our opinions
to roast men and women alive on account of them," wrote
Montaigne.

Hemingway was wrong when he said "What is moral is
what you feel good after, and what is immoral is what you feel
bad after." That moral theory, called emotivism (the "Boo-
Hooray theory")," was based simply on personal or group
approval or disapproval, which works, of course, only if you are
already civilized and have a well-developed conscience. (Ernie
felt good about killing a lion just for the fun of it, which could
be said of Attila the Hun after cutting off the heads of everybody
in an unfortunate town he invaded.)

In any case, morality does not require giving up the good
life, as Christian Fundamentalists believe, or even to be pious.
You can be moral and play poker at the same time, or be moral
and go to the racetrack (if you don't mind losing your money).
"Dost thou think because thou art virtuous, there shall be no
more cakes and ale?" asked Shakespeare. According to Russell,
"The fundamental defect of Christian ethics consists in the fact
that it labels certain classes of acts "sins" and others "virtues"
on the grounds that have nothing to do with their social conse-
quences." Whitehead asked "What is morality in any given
time or place? It is what the majority then and there happen to
like, and immorality is what they dislike."

To many sophisticated people, morality is a fake facade, a
social tool or posture. In the same vein, Twain said "An ethical
man is a Christian holding four aces." Mencken defined "conscience" very cynically as "the inner voice which reminds us

that someone may be looking." He ridiculed the religious approach to morality as follows: "Morality is the theory that every human act must either be right or wrong and that 99 percent of them are wrong."

Religion Is Often Immoral

Bernard J. Bamberger said "… the [Hebrew] Bible as we have it contains elements that are scientifically incorrect or even morally repugnant. No amount of "explaining away" can convince us that such passages are the product of Divine Wisdom." Obviously, morals can be bad for people if they are used mainly as a tool to advance religion. Shaw wrote: "An attack on morals may turn out to be the salvation of the race." It may well be that brothels exist because religion condemns normal sex. William Black wrote: "Prisons are built with stones of Law, Brothels with bricks of Religion."

Many people think that if they are religious they are automatically moral—as if you become smart if you put on a cap and gown! For example, pedophilia in the priesthood; killing infidels and innocent bystanders in the Crusades; burning nonbelievers at the stake, not only in Europe but in Massachusetts, where the Pilgrims burned the natives *alive* because they were *heathens*; praying for the poor instead of feeding them; banning books about sex and books with four-letter words even if they tell the truth; giving scholarships to the most religious instead of the smartest Catholic schoolchildren; fasting (how could fasting be moral or immoral?). How about giving your kids a religious education instead of a real education, handicapping them for the rest of their lives, (for example, teaching them "creationism," which makes your kids ignorant of science and the modern physical world—and distrustful of truly educated people). Currently, the political approach is that "moral relativism," as advocated and practiced by liberals, can't be moral.

Bloom wrote: "Value relativism can be taken to be a great

release from the perpetual tyranny of good and evil, with their cargo of shame and guilt, and the endless efforts that the pursuit of the one and avoidance of the other enjoin." Thus, morality is not a part of religion but a set of principles that must be applied on the basis of intelligence and self-interest.

The difference between religion and morality is illustrated starkly by Cardinal Newman in his Apologia: "Man ... rebelled against his Maker ... The Church must denounce rebellion as of all possible evils the greatest ... The Catholic Church holds it better for the sun and moon to drop from heaven, for the earth to fail, and for all the many millions on it to die of starvation in extremist agony ... than that one should ... commit one single venial sin, should tell one willful untruth, or should steal one farthing without excuse." That, of course, is religion in its most Moral (and thus immoral) form. Emerson's take was this: "We should not forgive the clergy for taking, on every issue, the immoral side."

"Sin is geographical," said Russell. Real morality, on the other hand, is much more basic and universal. "Morality consists in drawing the line somewhere," said an anonymous philosopher. Thus, a man who meets the Islamic moral standard may not meet the Christian or Jewish standard. Real morality, on the other hand, is much more basic and universal. According to *Daily Whale* on the Internet, here is a modern definition of morality as used by religionists for their own advantage: "Morality is the inimical force which attaches morals to so many of our otherwise serviceable stories, ruining them for all serious use ... ."

The Stoic school in ancient Greece, beginning in the third century *B.C.*, also taught that only those actions are morally correct for which *reasons* can be given, setting morality apart from religion. What is the reason for requiring a starving family to attend church services? Many Christians, full of guilt implanted by their preachers, think that morality is necessary because god sees everything, all the time, everywhere. A local radio broadcaster joked: "Hello, this is god. When I'm in Pittsburgh, which is all the time, I listen to all the local radio stations at once, including WRCT."

Most educated people agree with Ashley Montagu, who said "Evil is not inherent in nature: it is learned." Nietzsche put it more bluntly: "Morality is the best of all devices for leading mankind by the nose." Religious morality is not universal, but differs from place to place. In the same vein, Twain said "An ethical man is a Christian holding four aces." Mencken defined "conscience" very cynically as "the inner voice which reminds us that someone may be looking."

Like beauty, religious morality is in the eye of the beholder. For example, imagine that two Irishmen digging a ditch directly across from a brothel see a rabbi walk up to its front door, glance around and duck inside. "What's the world comin' to when men of the cloth are visitin' such places," said one. Later, a Protestant minister walks up to the door and quietly slips inside. "Why, it's no wonder the young people today are so confused," the digger said. Some time later, the men watched benignly as a Catholic priest furtively enters the house. "Ah, what a pity," the digger said, recognizing the priest, "one of the poor lasses must be ill." Religious people are easily confused about morality.

Kurtz wrote: "Theists today often bemoan the seeming decay of moral values in our society. Crime is rampant, and people are generally less concerned with the welfare of others than they seem to have been in generations past. The reasons for this are, of course, complex, but the theists themselves should be ready to take their share of the blame. For ages, the clergy have been drumming into people's heads the idea that "without god there is no ethics," and yet they are unable to produce evidence for their god and claims about god's will. *Thus, they are unable to produce what they insist is the foundation of ethics."* Since

nobody can agree on religion, it cannot be reasonable for morality to be religious either, as a matter of common sense.

Flew wrote: "... although a Creator might well torment
his creatures with reference to their having done what he must
have arranged that they should do, still creatures obviously cannot properly be held responsible to their Creator, precisely
because of what they are ... it is worth emphasizing once more
that the key notions here for Christian theism are those not of
morality and immorality but of sin and obedience ..." Morality
based upon human needs and social necessity can have a solid
foundation in both custom and logic. We know there can be a
dozen religious codes in America, but how could there be a
dozen moral codes, meaning codes of right and wrong? Does
America have a Catholic morality, a Fundamentalist Christian
morality, a Jewish morality, a more flexible Christian morality,
or what?

George Smith explained why religion is not morality as
follows: "... moral principles ... are subservient to human purposes ... In assessing the ethical significance of Jesus, it is illu-
minating to contrast him with the ancient Greek philosophers
who preceded him by hundreds of years. The differences are so
striking that few scholars care to place Jesus on the same level
as such intellectual giants as Plato and Aristotle ... To be
moral, according to Jesus, man must shackle his reason. He
must force himself to believe that which he cannot understand.
He must suppress, in the name of morality, any doubts that
surface in his mind." (Also, if god is really in control of our
lives, a person can make no moral judgments.) Smith said "...
we cannot blame or praise a man for an action over which he
has no control. Without volition, the Christian scheme of salvation is a farce ..."

Proudhon wrote: "Man is destined to live without religion, but the moral law is eternal and absolute. Who would
dare today to attack morality?"

But Isn't Morality About SEX?

"Wait a minute!" you're probably thinking, "WHAT ABOUT SEX?" Christian Fundamentalism was defined by some clever person as "the doctrine that there is an absolutely powerful, infinitely knowledgeable universe-spanning entity that is deeply and personally concerned about my sex life." "Considering all the evil that exists in the world, the fact that all of religion's condemnation is focused on expressing disapproval of two people loving each other proves just how evil religion is," said Jan de Boer. "Imagine using as an authority in the matter of marriage the opinion of a celibate priest!" said Joseph Lewis. In America, the main objection of religionists to birth control is that it is "against nature"—a lie meaning that it is "against religion." If so, then the Catholic *coitus interruptus*, as well as celibacy and chastity, should be immoral because they are against nature also.

Wilde said "The books that the world calls immoral are the books that show the world its own shame." Christian Fundamentalists condemn books that depict humans as they actually are because they want to shelter their children from reality. They use sex books with the genitals blanked out! Sex is normal for all mammals, while religion is something else. In fact, as today's headlines tell us, sex is normal for priests too! (The only thing abnormal here is the rules of celibacy and the choice of sexual partners, or victims.)

"Life is a sexually transmitted disease," said J.F. Hodge. Singer said "It is because those people who are regarded by the public as 'moral leaders of the community' have done so badly that morality, in the public mind, has come to mean a system of prohibitions against certain forms of sexual enjoyment." In his classic book, "Tradition," Professor Edward Shils wrote: "The tradition of Victorian morality as it grew in scope and adherence became too suffocating for a sensitive person to bear; it became insupportable." As we all know, nothing agitates a moralist more than a teen-aged girl in a miniskirt, flaunting some thigh. "And do you not think that each of you women is an Eve?" asked the blue-nosed Christian Tertullian, who thought women in general were shameless. "The judgment of God upon your sex endures even today; and with it inevitably endures your position of criminal at the bar of justice." The Koran says the same thing, which is why Muslim women have to cover everything but their eyes when out in public. Thus women are walking symbols of something shameful: human reproduction. Emerson said: "We should not forgive the clergy for taking, on every issue, the immoral side."

Why would a female want to be religious? Traditionally, the Christian religion has applied one standard (strict) to males and another standard (impossibly strict) to females. Devout Christian males always treat females as subordinates, if not servants. One can only conclude that Arab and Christian Fundamentalist women have no mind of their own, and like it that way. "As long as woman regards the Bible as the charter of her rights, she will be the slave of man. The Bible was not written by a woman. Within its leaves there is nothing but humiliation and shame for her," said Ingersoll a long time ago. Freud said "Sexual morality, as society defines it, is contemptible."

The big rallies held by the Christian "Promise Keepers" feature pledges by husbands to love and protect their wives *in exchange for their servitude*! In India and other non-industrialized countries, where the average human life span is under 50, it is normal and reasonable for girls to marry at age 14. Most civilized countries leave it to individual families to determine things such as type of conduct permissible for minors, including clothing, mixed sex activities, dancing, etc., and pre-marital sex. But rules for such things have never been regarded as applicable on a consistent basis to all segments of the U.S. population. There are liberal families and there are conservative families. "Sex and obscenity are not synonymous," ruled the

U.S. Supreme Court (*Roth* case), as some religious nuts think.

Even in America, the well-to-do classes have always granted themselves moral license to live a little faster and freer than the working classes, even though they invariably prescribe religion as necessary for those classes. In religious countries, particularly Muslim countries, on the other hand, state officials intervene constantly in sexual matters. In the Massachusetts Colony prior to the American Revolution, it is well known that governmental officials intervened in sexual matters and punished those whose sexual conduct was considered outside of the strict puritanical ethical code. But the lower economic classes in America have now become as promiscuous as the upper classes always were. Religious morality is form over substance. As the Chinese call-girl pronounced (with a typical Chinese accent) when she got her marriage license, "It won't be wrong now."

Norman Douglas said "Chastity is an insult to the Creator and an abomination to man and beast." Aldous Huxley defined chastity as: "the most unnatural of the sexual perversions," and he referred to continence as "that melancholy sexual perversion." On the other hand, Gibbon said "To a philosophic eye the vices of the clergy are far less dangerous than their virtues." Also, as Mencken said, "It is now quite lawful for a Catholic woman to avoid pregnancy by a resort to mathematics, though she is still forbidden to resort to physics or chemistry." Freud said "Sexual morality, as society defines it, is contemptible." Shaw asked "Why should we take advice on sex from the pope? If he knows anything about it, he shouldn't."

Christian Fundamentalism was defined by some clever person as "the doctrine that there is an absolutely powerful, infinitely knowledgeable universe-spanning entity that is deeply and personally concerned about my sex life." Wilde said "The books that the world call immoral are the books that show the world its own shame." In any case, religious rules are not strong enough to change the sexuality of human animals. "The Anglo-Saxon conscience does not prevent the Anglo-Saxon from sinning; it merely prevents him from enjoying his sin," said Salvador de Madariaga. "Religion has done love a great service by making it a sin," said Anatole France. Christian Fundamentalists are so afraid of premarital sex that they supervise and chaperone teenagers and forbid dancing. As the old joke goes, "Why don't Baptists make love standing up? Because they are afraid it will lead to dancing."

As for books and magazines about sexual matters, the same approach applies. "There is no such thing as a moral or immoral book. Books are well written or badly written," said Wilde and hundreds of other people (and American judges). Is sex dirty? "Only if it's done right," said Woody Allen.

Butch Hancock said "Life in Lubbock, Texas taught me two things. One is that God loves you and you're going to burn in hell. The other is that sex is the most awful, dirty thing on the face of the earth and you should save it for someone you love." As for entertainment in any form, Tertullian was afraid of that, too: "There is no public entertainment which does not inflict spiritual damage," he said.

In a paper on "Sexual Abuse in Christian Homes and Churches," Carolyn H. Heggen wrote: "A disturbing fact continues to surface in sex abuse research. The first best predictor of abuse is alcohol or drug addiction in the father. But the second best predictor is conservative religiosity, accompanied by parental belief in traditional male-female roles. This means that if you want to know which children are most likely to be sexually abused by their father, the second most significant clue is whether or not the parents belong to a conservative religious group with traditional role beliefs and rigid sexual attitudes." (There are good reasons why conservative religious people oppose sociology and sociologists who investigate and publish facts like that.)

Religion Is Often Immoral

Emerson's take was this: "We should not forgive the clergy for taking, on every issue, the immoral side." Since nobody can agree on religion, it cannot be reasonable for morality to be religious either, as a matter of common sense.

Contrary to what the preachers say, Americans are a moral people, as compared with people of most other places or times. In sixteenth century Italy, the daughter of Galileo was illegitimate. As was the custom in those quaint, "moral" days, she was sent to a convent in order to atone for her father's sin of not marrying the mother. In those days, religion and politics were the same thing. "Politics has no relation to morals," said Machiavelli (who was in a good position to see that kind of stuff at firsthand). "I like convents, but I wish they wouldn't admit any women under the age of fifty," said Napoleon Bonaparte.

Horace Walpole asked "Tell me, ye divines, which is the most virtuous man, he who begets twenty bastards, or he who sacrifices an hundred thousand lives?" Religious morality can be just as hypocritical as cultural morality, as shown by the contemporary practice of Italian and other European priests of keeping sexual mistresses, as discussed recently by the Catholic intellectual Garry Wills. Shaw wrote: "An attack on morals may turn out to be the salvation of the race," meaning that current morals are hypocritical and even damaging. Macauley pointed out that "the Puritans banned bear-baiting, not because it gave pain to the bear, but because it gave pleasure to the spectators."

Civilization Depends On Secular Morality

"The problem is how to construct a world in which immoral people can do the least harm; not how to enable moral people to do the most good," said Milton Friedman. "The greatest happiness of the greatest number is the foundation of morality and legislation," said Jeremy Bentham. Singer said there are two simple moral and ethical premises: "The first is the existence of our ability to reason. The second is that, in reasoning about practical matters, we are able to distance ourselves from our own point of view and take on, instead, a wider perspective; ultimately even the point of view of the universe. Reason makes it possible for us to see ourselves in this way because, by thinking about my place in the world, I am able to see that I am just one being among others, with interests and desires like others … reason enables me to see that they have similarly subjective perspectives, and that from the point of view of the universe my perspective is no more privileged than theirs." Charles Bradlaugh wrote in 1864: "Atheists would teach men to be moral now, not because God offers as an inducement reward by and by, but because in the virtuous act itself immediate good is insured to the doer and the circle surrounding him."

Morality deals with good and bad acts by individuals, and nothing more. It is not a *group* thing, but a *personal* thing. You cannot point to a church picnic and say those people are moral, and then point to golfers on a Sunday and say those people are not. How about just obeying the law, which is a community's moral command? The more religious people are, the less important they think law is! "I answer to a higher power," is their sad cop-out! We know there can be a dozen religious codes in America, but how could there be a dozen moral codes?

Democracy Is An Aspect Of Morality

Many scholars think that modern non-religious morality began in the Enlightenment with Thomas Hobbes, who is credited with the idea that secular considerations come first, and that morals relate to individual human rights. He wrote that individual human psychology, rather than exterior standards, determines what is moral and that individualism and the acquisitive, worldly mode of life is therefore "respectable" instead of "immoral." *In effect, he made capitalism okay for Christians, and should be honored by every Chamber of*

Commerce in America. Every man seeks pleasure and the avoidance of pain, he wrote. "Good" means either pleasure or the objects which are sources of pleasure. The basic social interest is to harness the forward energies of men instead of dealing with religion-based moral obstacles, said Hobbes.

In a democracy, laws that are approved by a majority in accordance with custom are generally accepted as ethical or moral. Taxes and punishments for crime are ethical if a majority approve them for the general welfare. Laws regulating conduct are also accepted as ethical and moral for the same reason. Whitehead wrote: "Moral codes have suffered from the exaggerated claims made for them. The dogmatic fallacy has here done its worst. Each such code has been put out by a god on a mountain top, or by a saint in a cave, or by a divine despot on a throne, or, at the lowest, by ancestors with a wisdom beyond later question. In any case, each code is incapable of improvement; and unfortunately in details they fail to agree either with each other or with our existing moral intuitions." *An absolute command to act or not act in a certain way cannot produce justice for all parties.*

We all know that, under peculiar circumstances, murder and robbery can not only be justified but defended as a moral duty. The German generals who tried to kill Hitler were acting morally and ethically, even though they were disobeying the Ten Commandments. ("But how can I kill Adolf? I'm a Catholic! *You* do it, Carl, because you're an atheist!")

In America, the Christian Right wants us to follow the example of the Muslim world in enforcing literally the commandments of a "holy book" instead of common sense! In other words, we should stand up for our American religion like they do, and just blow our enemies to hell! It is hard to see, after 9/11, how people could fail to see the dangers in taking religion seriously.

Thus, the Constitution is a far greater source and example of morality than the Bible. It is now the closest thing there is to applied Utilitarianism, the philosophy of Locke and Mill: the pursuit of happiness that leads to the greatest good for the greatest number. Religionists are fond of saying that the Constitution is fine as far as it goes, dealing with things like voting, etc., but is deficient in the area of morals, which can only be supplied by religion. In fact, the Declaration of Independence and Constitution represent the thinking of the most advanced philosophers of the Enlightenment in the field of ethics, morals and government. *The Constitution is, among other things, a set of moral standards. To be a model American citizen is thus by definition a moral and ethical matter, whether one believes in god or not.* The American Constitution has been admired by scholars the world over for over two centuries, and copied by dozens of other countries not ruled by religious demagogues.

According to scholars and encyclopedia writers, the Constitution ranks with the teachings of Plato, Aristotle, Confucius and other highly regarded philosophers as a foundation for morality and ethics. The Constitution was the first document of its kind to be based upon contemporary philosophical thinkers (Locke and Mill) and not upon tradition. It was a complete break from the laws of England, France and Germany.

Bentham, Locke, Mill and other great moral philosophers equated morality with a system of utilitarian laws that would, if followed, produce the greatest good for the greatest number. They insisted upon providing a good life for the common man, which in their time was a revolutionary idea, and which provides the foundation for our Constitution. The Constitution is a far greater source and example of morality than the Christian Bible.

Morals Have Evolved Genetically With Humans

Contemporary thinkers tell us that morals are the means and the necessary result of human evolution, starting from prehistoric times. In his book *The Moral Animal,* Robert Wright challenged the accepted sociological idea that human nature is merely the material that "social factors" mold and transform. (Christians are constantly telling us things like, "We are here on Earth to help others." Carlin asks "If so, what are the others here for?") Wright also challenged the idea of the psychologist-philosopher B.F. Skinner that the human animal is merely the product of social conditioning and nothing more. What really evolved, he said, was a "developmental program" in our brains that absorbs information from experience and adjusted to it *so we could survive.* Nobody will ever know whether we would have survived if we had reacted differently to nature. We could have been like dinosuars: extinct.

Wright said *"Altruism, compassion, empathy, love, conscience, the sense of justice—all of these things, the things that hold society together, the things that allow our species to think so highly of itself, can be confidently said to have a firm genetic basis.* That's the good news. The bad news is that, although these things are in some ways blessings for humanity as a whole, they didn't evolve for the good of the species, and aren't reliably employed to that end." Wright's ideas are part of what is known as "evolutionary biology" and "evolutionary psychology," holding that the human brain and emotional system have evolved, along with the rest of the body, to have certain characteristics that favor survival. *In other words, if we hadn't acted morally in the past, we wouldn't be here as a species.*

Evolutionary biology, naturally enough, embodies the theories of Darwin. The closest thing to a generic Darwinian view of how moral codes arise is this, said Wright: "... *people tend to pass the sorts of moral judgments that help move their genes into the next generation."*

In other words, what you see is what you get, and "that is all there is, there isn't any more." If Wright is right, all this fuss about morality may be useless and beside the point: just by surviving and continuing to evolve, we will automatically be moral creatures! If human beings were not basically moral, we'd all be dead!

What has that got to do with morality? Well, it explains what morality is and what morality is not. It explains that we can have morality without a god or religion, because morality is something inherent in the human mind and instincts. Even certain animals, like apes and dogs, have a morality that prevents them from killing and eating their own relatives.

CHAPTER 5

WHAT IS RELIGION?

"We are all tattooed in our cradles with the beliefs of our tribe; the record may seem superficial, but it is indelible. You cannot educate a man wholly out of the superstitious fears which were implanted in his imagination, no matter how utterly his reason may reject them."

—Oliver Wendell Holmes (Sr.)

"Waiter!" called an irate diner: "What is the meaning of this fly in my soup?" The waiter answered, "I don't know, sir, I'm a waiter, not a priest."

Religion Explains (Incorrectly) How The World Works

In prehistoric times, scholars tell us, everyday occurrences of all kinds were given mystical meanings by tribal priests. If some catastrophe ensued just when a fly landed in the king's soup, a priest or shaman was called upon to explain it. James G. Frazer, in *The Golden Bough*, defined religion as being "a propitiation or conciliation of powers superior to man which are believed to direct and control the course of nature and of human life." Durkheim said "The god of the clan, the totemic principle, can therefore be nothing else than the clan itself, personified and represented to the imagination under the visible form of the animal or vegetable which serves as totem." Hocart said "If we turn to the living myth ... we find that it has no existence apart from the ritual ..."

According to scholars, the Bible and the Christian religion were created haphazardly by thousands of people, most of them unknown, during the early centuries following the death of Jesus. "An honest God is the noblest work of man," said Ingersoll. "Man has created God, not God man," said Garibaldi. He also said: "The priest is the personification of falsehood." Russell said "God and Satan alike are essentially human figures, the one a projection of ourselves, the other of our enemies." Voltaire wrote: "Superstition, born of paganism and adopted by Judaism, has infested the Christian Church from earliest times."

"It is only the savage, whether of the African bush or the American gospel tent, who pretends to know the will and intent of god exactly and completely," said Mencken. "The first priest was the first knave who met the first fool," said Voltaire. Montaigne said "It comes to pass that nothing is so firmly believed as that which we know least; nor are there any persons so sure of themselves as those who tell us fables, such as alchemists, prognosticators, seers, chiromantics, quacks, id genus omne."

Baron d'Holbach, who was guillotined in the French revolution, said "If we go back to the beginning we shall find that ignorance and fear created the gods, that fancy, enthusiasm, or deceit adorned or disfigured them; that weakness worships them; that credulity preserves them and that custom, respect, and tyranny support them in order to make the blindness of man serve its own interests." Voltaire said "If God did not exist, it would be necessary to invent Him." Russell said "We may define "faith" as a firm belief in something for which there is no evidence. When there is evidence, no one speaks of "faith" ... We do not speak of a faith that two and two are four or that the earth is round." Luther said: *"Faith must trample under foot all reason, sense, and understanding." Religion, to Luther, was not only the most important thing, it was the only important thing* (sounding like Vince Lombardi).

Increase Mather, father of Cotton Mather, said "Thunder is the voice of God, and, therefore, to be dreaded." Levi-Straus (no relation to the jeans people) said the purpose of myth is "to provide a logical model capable of overcoming a contradiction." "All gods are homemade, and it is we who pull their strings, and so give them the power to pull ours," said A. Huxley. Imagined beings become part of reality (as when the bartender suddenly sees a pink elephant at the bar: "You're a little early, Jumbo—that customer hasn't come in yet.")

"The dice of God are always loaded," said Emerson. Levi-Straus said the purpose of myth is "to provide a logical model capable of overcoming a contradiction," meaning something not otherwise explainable. More recently, Woody Allen said "I believe there is something out there watching over us. Unfortunately, it's the Government."

The trappings of religion, such as costumes, symbols, music, art and architecture, are at least as important to believers as the dogma. "When Art was born, Religion took possession of it," said Saint-Saens. Montaigne said "Catholicism is paganism spiritualized." Hobbes said "The papacy is no other than the ghost of the deceased Roman Empire, sitting crowned upon the grave thereof."

Yet priests and pastors still carry on the tradition of simplistic, but wrong, learning. Pascal said "Men never do evil so completely and cheerfully as when they do it from religious conviction." Santayana said "Religion is valid poetry infused into common life. It is not revelation truer than perception or than science." In recent times, Tillich became famous for thinking that religion helped people get through life even though it is false!

Santayana wrote: "Christianity persecuted, tortured, and burned. Like a hound it tracked the very scent of heresy. It kindled wars, and nursed furious hatreds and ambitions. It sanctified, quite like Mohameddism, extermination and tyranny. All this would have been impossible if, like Buddhism, it had looked only for peace and the liberation of souls. It looked beyond; it dreamt of infinite blisses and crowns it should be crowned with before an electrified universe and an applauding God ... Buddhism had tried to quiet a sick world with anesthetics; Christianity sought to purge it with fire."

Meaning

Today religion continues to provide something called "meaning" even though it is often at odds with what we now perceive as "reality." Maugham said "Now the answer ... is plain, but it is so unpalatable that most men will not face it. There is no reason for life and life has no meaning." Ex-minister Dan Barker said "Not thinking critically, I assumed that the "successful" prayers were proof that god answers prayer while the failures were proof that there was something wrong with me." Kafka said "The meaning of life is that it stops," meaning that life must be lived to the hilt while we are alive. "Religion attracts more devotion according as it demands more faith— that is to say, as it becomes more incredible to the profane mind," said Amiel. He also said "The philosopher aspires to explain away all mysteries, to dissolve them into light ... Mystery, on the other hand, is demanded and pursued by the religious instinct; mystery constitutes the essence of worship." Religion has created something called "evil" in order to justify god. Conrad wrote: "The belief in a supernatural source of evil is not necessary; men alone are quite capable of every wickedness."

There Is No Such Thing As "Meaning" Apart From Events

Wittgenstein explained that events regarded as random happenings can have no meaning because meaning consists only of the thoughts of two or more people who agree on some particular idea. *Thus, "meaning" is not transferable, like a dollar bill, although preachers never stop trying to tell you what a hurricane "means."* In fact, the Bible "means" only what each reader thinks it means, and is otherwise devoid of meaning.

To this day you can see groups of relatives of the TWA Flight 800 victims on the Long Island beach placing wreaths, etc., sharing some kind of collective "transcendental" or "holistic" experience. They are unwilling to believe that something like that could possibly happen by chance: "Why were all of *our* relatives killed?" If your kid's bike chain breaks and injures him, you accept that normally, as part of the law of averages; you don't say "Why was the bike of *my kid* defective?"

Almost every day there is an article in some newspaper with a headline like "After 7 Are Killed, Texans Look for Meaning." That article reported that, after a gunman killed seven people at a night prayer service, hundreds of people crowded the churches. "I think his father dying left a big hole," a plumber said about the killer, thinking normally and logically. "It's a sign we're getting close to the end of time," a seminary student said, echoing several others who spoke of signs of the apocalypse. "A collective search for meaning is under way here, among strangers drawn to give their blood to help those wounded," wrote the reporter.

The bombing of the Federal Building in Oklahoma City, another random act, is now a major "religious event," like the destruction of the cult headquarters in Waco, Texas, and now, the Twin Towers. Relatives of the deceased always believe that god had something to do with those meaningless deaths for the simple reason that god (they believe) was "in charge of" the happening. Religious leaders, as they always have, exploit these kinds of events for their own gain in power and wealth, by insisting that god (or god's enemies) caused it. Pat Robertson and Jerry Falwell jointly announced, right after the Twin Towers collapse (seizing the opportunity to make headlines), *that it was caused by god because Americans, who tolerate homosexuality, immorality, and womens' rights, etc. are not religious enough!* On the contrary, Goethe said "Mysteries are not necessarily miracles."

Rousseau wrote: "Christianity preaches only servitude and dependence. Its spirit is so favorable to tyranny that it always profits by such a regime. *True Christians are made to be slaves, and they know it and do not much mind; this short life counts for too little in their eyes.*" According to Schleirmacher, the effect of the Enlightenment on religion was to make religion "merely an instinct craving for a mess of metaphysical and moral crumbs, instead of the seat of all human knowledge ... For, in the first place, it [Enlightenment] is disinterested ... The religions, which deal in promises and threats regarding a future life, do exactly the contrary; they fasten down the thoughts to the person's own posthumous interests ..." Unfortunately, only educated people know that the Enlightenment was a revolt against religion.

Americans are just as gullible as medieval Europeans. Disk jockey Don Imus used to begin his radio program with his "Plastic Jesus" song, as follows: "I don't care if it rains or freezes / 'long as I got my plastic Jesus / Sittin' on the dashboard of my car / It makes no difference if we hit a bump / He's held on by a suction cup / Sittin' on the dashboard of my car ..." There is an old saying: "What men usually ask from god when they pray is that two and two not make four." They want the world to be changed just for them! They would rather pray for the real rules of the universe *not* to work than to adapt their lives to reality by moving to higher ground. "Convictions are more dangerous foes of truth than lies," said Nietzsche.

Pinker said "For anyone with a persistent intellectual curiosity, religious explanations are not worth knowing because they pile equally baffling enigmas on top of the original ones." Bernard Berenson said "Miracles happen to those who believe in them. Otherwise why does not the Virgin Mary appear to Lamaists, Mohammedans, or Hindus who have never heard of her?" It requires only two things to win credit for a miracle: a mountebank and a number of silly women," said de Sade.

Einstein said "I cannot imagine a god who rewards and punishes the objects of his creation, whose purposes are moulded after our own—a god, in short, who is but a reflection of human frailty. Neither do I believe that the individual survives the death of his body, although feeble souls harbor such thoughts through fear of ridiculous egotisms." Pinker wrote: "As the Yiddish expression goes, if god lived on earth, people would break his windows." "If man had created man," said Mark Twain, "he would be ashamed of his performance." "Don't blame god: he's only human," said Leo Rosten. L. Ron Hubbard, founder of the "Scientology" religious-business scam, said "It is convenient that there be gods and, as it is convenient, let us believe that there are." (He allegedly also said "If you want to make a million … the quickest way is to start your own religion.")

Christopher Morley, for example, said "My theology, briefly, is that the universe was dictated but not signed." Tillich said "All mythological elements in the Bible, the doctrine and liturgy, should be recognized as mythological, but they should be maintained in their symbolic form and not be replaced by scientific substitutes." In other words, religion "works" because it is symbolic, and the symbolism alone (true or not) is all that is required to make people feel secure. *"We should always be disposed to believe that that which appears to us to be white is really black, if the hierarchy of the Church so decides," said St. Ignatius of Loyola.*

Cardinal Newman said "From the age of fifteen, dogma

has been the fundamental principle of my religion: I know no other religion; I cannot enter into the idea of any other sort of religion; religion, as a mere sentiment, is to me a dream and a mockery." Ben Franklin said "The way to see by Faith is to shut the Eye of Reason." Voltaire wrote: "A wise and courageous prince, with money, troops, and laws, can perfectly well govern men without the aid of religion, which was made only to deceive them; but the stupid people would soon make one for themselves, and as long as there are fools and rascals there will be religions." "Men never do evil so completely and cheerfully as when they do it from religious conviction," said Pascal. Of course, the by-products of religion are as valued by religionists as the religion itself, such as music, art, architecture, paintings of the Virgin Mary, etc. ("People may say what they like about the decay of Christianity; the religious system that produced green Chartreuse can never really die," wrote Saki.)

Religion offers something no other idea can offer: 100 per cent certainty, whether fallible or infallible. Montaigne said "It comes to pass that nothing is so firmly believed as that which we know least; nor are there any persons so sure of themselves as those who tell us fables, such as alchemists, prognosticators, seers, chiromantics, quacks, *id genus omne.* To which I would join, if I dared, a host of persons, interpreters and verifiers-in-ordinary of the designs of God."

Hugo wrote: "Religion is nothing but the shadow cast by the universe on human intelligence." *"Anything which is rational is always difficult for the lay mind. But the thing which is irrational anyone can understand.* That is why religion came so early into the world," wrote Chesterton. "The Catholics and the Communists are alike in assuming that an opponent cannot be both honest and intelligent," said Orwell. Russell said "God and Satan alike are essentially human figures, the one a projection of ourselves, the other of our enemies." Joyce Carol Oates said "Homo sapiens is the species that invents symbols in which to invest passion and authority, then forgets that symbols are inventions."

Christianity thrived during medieval times on *inherently unbelievable* tales of martyrs. Shaw said "Martyrdom is the only way in which a man can become famous without ability." "A thing is not necessarily true because a man dies for it," said Wilde and a thousand other people. Nehru said "I want nothing to do with any religion concerned with keeping the masses satisfied to live in hunger, filth, and ignorance." Leo Rosten said "Don't blame God: he's only human." Mark Twain said "If man had created man, he would be ashamed of his performance." "No actual tyrant known to history has ever been guilty of one hundredth of the crimes, massacres, and other atrocities attributed to the Deity in the Bible," said Steve Allen. Religion now divides people instead of uniting them (like the proverbial Vatican Airlines that printed its escape instructions in Latin so Catholics could escape first).

Another reason why religion survives in the scientific, democratic age is that poorly educated people can be easily fooled by the warped "logic" used by religionists to "prove" its authenticity. For example, religionists regularly attempt to argue that one's inability to *see* spiritual force is meaningless in the case of "invisible beings!" (A satirist wrote: "Like all religions, the Holy Religion of the Invisible Pink Unicorn is based upon both Logic and Faith. We have Faith that She is Pink; *and we Logically know that She is Invisible, because we can't see Her."*) Mencken said "We must respect the other fellow's religion, but only in the same sense and to the extent that we respect his theory that his wife is beautiful and his children smart."

How Do Pointy-headed Intellectuals Explain Religion?

As Martin Luther said many times, religion is intended to take the place of thinking by the masses. Orthodox Russians and Catholics literally worship statues and pictures of saints and Jesus, which takes them out of the present world and places them in an imaginary one. (J.E. Larrson quipped "How do you get fresh air in a Russian church? You click on one of the icons.") Of course, Americans do not know what the martyrs, Mary, or god really looked like, except, of course, that images of God must bear some family resemblance to Jesus, his son. Nobody knows what Jesus looked like either, except that he certainly was not a Nordic type, as the rural Christians now believe. Scientists tell us he looked like today's Palestinians— Yassir Arafat, for example. If the hard-core, unschooled conservatives knew that, they would stop being Christians. They are like the little girl in school who said she was drawing a picture of god. "No one knows what god really looks like," said the teacher. "They will in a minute," answered the girl."

"A thing is not necessarily true because a man dies for it," said Wilde and a thousand other people. Albert Einstein said "I cannot imagine a God who rewards and punishes the objects of his creation, whose purposes are moulded after our own—a God, in short, who is but a reflection of human frailty." Religion is like the old real estate con game, describing in exact detail places that don't exist. Gloria Steinem said "It's an incredible con job when you think of it, to believe something now in exchange for life after death. Even corporations with all their reward systems don't try to make it posthumous."

In all religions, god was in charge of every detail of human life. "The dice of god are always loaded," said Emerson in all seriousness, meaning that, if you believe in god, everything bad or good that happens is manipulated by god. Einstein said: "I cannot imagine a god who rewards and punishes the objects of his creation, whose purposes are moulded after our own—a god, in short, who is but a reflection of human frailty. Neither do I believe that the individual survives the death of his body, although feeble souls harbor such thoughts through fear of ridiculous egotisms." Even Tillich dismissed belief in the after-life as "a corrupt form of theological expression, disseminated among the relatively poor and uneducated." "Humankind cannot bear much reality," said T.S. Eliot.

Bentham said "But in truth, in no instance has a system in regard to religion been ever established, but for the purpose, as well as with the effect of its being made an instrument of intimidation, corruption, and delusion, for the support of depredation and oppression in the hands of government." Hume said "In all ages of the world, priests have been enemies of liberty."

As Burke said, "Superstition is the religion of feeble minds." How can it still be justified? Carlin said "Religion is sort of like a lift in your shoes. If it makes you feel better, fine. Just don't ask me to wear your shoes." Susan B. Anthony said "I distrust those people who know so well what God wants them to do because I notice it always coincides with their own desires." Some Internet sage said: "Christianity is like renting two videos—Bambi and Dracula—and trying to combine them into something intelligible."

Turgenev said "Whatever a man prays for, he prays for a miracle. Every prayer reduces itself to this: "Great God, grant that twice two not be four." Bloom said people must fight for something they intellectually know is not true in order to have "culture," *i.e. something identified with them as a group.* A shared sense of "the sacred" is the surest way to recognize a culture, he said, *because the religious experience is the thing, not god.* In the twentieth century, he said, tradition was regarded by highly educated people as the cause and the consequence of "ignorance, superstition, clerical dominance, religious intolerance, social hierarchy, inequality, birth status and other states of mind which were the objects of rationalistic censure."

Religion has always been used to justify immoral conduct that benefits people in power. "There is not one verse in the

Bible inhibiting slavery, but many regulating it. It is not then, we conclude, immoral," said Rev. Alexander Campbell. Darwin said "For my part I would as soon be descended from a baboon … as from a savage who delights to torture his enemies, treats his wives like slaves, and is haunted by the grossest superstitions."

All religions, of course, provide some valuable secular benefits to somebody, if not to everybody, in order to stay in business. "Every man thinks God is on his side. The rich and powerful know he is," said Anouilh. "The Good Lord gave me my money," explained John D. Rockefeller. Bernard Katz described organized religion as "The world's largest pyramid scheme." It takes two people, of course, to play the religious scam. "The only person who is a worse liar than a faith healer is his patient," said Lincoln (a non-religious person). The church, of course, encourages that way of looking at the uncertainty of life. "Randomness scares people, said Fran Liebowitz. "Religion is a way to explain randomness." Pinker wrote: "If you can convince your children that your soul will live on and watch over their affairs, they are less emboldened to defect while you are alive."

Of course, no religion is rigidly and consistently followed. Bierce defined a Christian as "one who follows the teachings of Christ in so far as they are not inconsistent with a life of sin." Thus even sinners can support their local religion because it allows them to sin now and then, which is the generally recognized genius of Catholic Church confessions. Non-Fundamentalist Protestant religionists tend to modernize their religion, to keep it up to date and thus more user-friendly. According to Newsprayer.com, radio beams can be sent to God's last known residence, being the site of the Big Bang, which has now been located in outer space. (The rate was $5.00 per prayer, six pre-paid prayers for $25, which is similar to the Catholic rate for special prayers.)

Religion And Tradition Are The Same Thing

Dickens said "I believe the spreading of Catholicism to be the most horrible means of political and social degradation left in the world." "Religion is what keeps the poor from murdering the rich," said Napoleon. "I want nothing to do with any religion concerned with keeping the masses satisfied to live in hunger, filth, and ignorance," said Nehru. "The Catholics and the Communists are alike in assuming that an opponent cannot be both honest and intelligent," said Orwell.

Tradition does not mean that the living are dead; it means that the dead are living," said Harold MacMillan, a traditionalist. In his landmark book, *Tradition*, Professor Edward Shils said that tradition is what, "having been created through human actions, through thought and imagination, is handed down from one generation to the next ... It includes all that a society of a given time possesses and which already existed when its present possessors came upon it." A sense of filiation or continuity is a sense of being "connected" with an unbroken chain of generations which have some significant quality in common. Also, he wrote: "Substantive traditionality, i.e., the appreciation of the accomplishments and wisdom of the past ... is one of the major patterns of human thought ... Human beings have to adhere to some beliefs; it is not in their nature to do otherwise ... They must believe something about the world in which they live, both about what they see and what they do not see ... Tradition offers to the present things created and set going in the past; these things include beliefs—scientific and scholarly knowledge, religious beliefs, conceptions of the right order of society, norms of conduct in private and public life." It cannot be wiped out; it can only change slowly.

"Tradition means giving votes to the most obscure of all classes, our ancestors," said Chesterton. "When custom and reason are at odds, custom always wins out," said Napoleon. Shils acknowledged that a "traditional society is no more a reign of virtue than the societies which have been affected by the notion that traditions were hindrances to improvement ... Rulers were frequently rapacious, wars were cruel, priests were often not virtuous, outbursts of violence and fanaticism were recurrent."

Thus religion can always be relied upon to justify social wrongdoing. *The misery and strife that is tearing the world apart right now is caused by religion: Muslim against Jew; Muslim against Christian; Sunni Muslim against Shiite Muslim.* Who cannot logically say that the Twin Tower horror was an example of "religion in action?" All religions are alike in that they have the potential to get out of control and cause great harm. As a matter of history and logic, it might be argued that the Crusades were the Christian equivalent of September 11, 2001; we destroy their civilization, they destroy ours. (Muslim fundamentalists have long memories.)

Religion Is Conformity

"The race of men, while sheep in credulity, are wolves for conformity," Carl Van Doren reminded us. A sociologist named Asch conducted some famous experiments to show how conformity works among college students, who are inclined to side with the majority on any issue. Churches, even in America, have always protested the teaching *in public schools* of ideas that tend to diverge from church teaching. Benjamin Jowett, a famous British schoolmaster, said to one of his pupils "You will find God by tomorrow morning, or leave this college." Frank Zappa said "What was it that Adam ate that he wasn't supposed to eat? It wasn't just an apple. It was the fruit of the Tree of Knowledge of Good and Evil. The subtle message? 'Get smart and I'll fuck you over,' sayeth the Lord. God is the smartest, and he doesn't want any competition. Is this not an absolutely anti-intellectual religion?"

It makes no difference whether a religion is "rational" or

"nonrational," because it serves that social purpose either way. Fundamentalists confuse what is real with what goes on in their heads, where everything they can imagine is real. According to an old joke, when the preacher gets insomnia, it's because the sheep he was counting fell asleep. They are like the lion who complained to his psychiatrist that every time he roared he had to sit through a two-hour movie.

Another example of that is the warning Oral Roberts once gave to his flock that god might "call him back" if his current financial drive was unsuccessful. Reality and unreality are all the same to a Christian Fundamentalist! It is mainly the Catholics and Fundamentalists in America who brag that their god is superior to the gods of other religions, which is like saying, "My teddy bear can beat up your teddy bear." (Maybe so, but it can't beat up atheist teddy bears, which, presumably, are not imaginary.)

We have clearly reached the point where religion is not only incompatible with many aspects of American culture, and beyond: *religion is now actually opposing, with all its money and power, current scientific knowledge and rational thinking.* A majority of the American people reject the teachings of science and its measurements of reality. Goaded on by uneducated congressmen like Tom Delay, they are at present trying to force public schools and universities to teach something called "creationism" instead of biology, physics and geology! Most parents seem to be saying: "That's not my problem!" Durkheim recognized that *religion is itself a unique kind of reality for people who otherwise could not understand the world.* The last people to give up religion will be the uneducated and unintelligent ones, he said.

Bakunin, sounding like a commentator on our current political scene, wrote: "Nothing is more natural than that the belief in God, the creator, regulator, judge, master, curser, savior, and benefactor of the world, should still prevail among the people, especially in the rural districts, where it is more wide-spread than among the proletariat of the cities. The people, unfortunately, are still very ignorant, and are kept in ignorance by the systematic effort of all the governments, who consider this ignorance, not without good reason, as one of the essential conditions of their own power ..." (Does the Republican National Committee read Bakunin?)

Abandonment Of Tradition Is Also Traditional

Eventually, however, Shils says that "the 'dynamic' ideal in Western societies requires departures from traditional ways of seeing and doing things ... It is an expression of discontent with what has been received ... The discontent focuses concretely on the insufficiency in the amount of material well-being enjoyed by individuals." *This process has come to be known as the "rationalization" of society, meaning the process of weeding out inconsistent, older values and institutions that is going on now in America.* "The idea of progress presents the latest form of society as better than earlier forms ... This conception is itself a rejection of the value of any patterns of action called tradition," said Shils. "We want to live in the present and the only history that is worth a tinker's damn is the history we make today," said Henry Ford. Similarly, Toynbee said "Civilization is a movement and not a condition, a voyage and not a harbor."

Although one of the effects of rationalization is "emancipation" from traditional restrictions on personal freedom and individual rights, only the moderately educated middle classes seem to perceive it this way. In recent years churchmen have "modernized" ceremonial procedures to encourage attendance. If they go too far, of course, it would take the mystery out of the service. (Some jokester said that, if low-fat communion wafers are developed, parishioners might say things like: "I can't *believe* it's not really Jesus!") That does not mean that tradition is 100 per cent "good," Shils said. "The treatment of the Bible as just another book in recent times encountered many resistances from the proponents of the tradition ..."

Social Class

As Leo Tolstoy explained, most educated people today live without faith: "On the one hand the minority of wealthy, educated people, having freed themselves from the hypnotism of the Church, believe in nothing. They look upon all faiths as absurdities or as useful means of keeping the masses in bondage—no more. On the other hand, the vast majority, poor, uneducated, but for the most part truly sincere, remain under the hypnotism of the faith. But this is not really faith, for instead of throwing light on man's position in the world it only darkens it."

Shaw wrote: "Indeed, the religious bodies, as the almoners of the rich, become a sort of auxiliary police, taking off the insurrectionary edge of poverty with coals and blankets, bread and treacle, and soothing and cheering the victims with hopes of immense and inexpensive happinesses in another world when the process of working them to premature death in the service of the rich is complete in this."

Upton Sinclair (once considered a dangerous radical) said "From the days of Constantine to the days of Bismarck and Mark Hanna, Christ and Caesar have been one, and the Church has been the shield and armor of predatory economic might." That explains why the wealthy (who otherwise tend to be more sophisticated) seek the support of the Christian Fundamentalists, who are so tacky, uncouth, naive and unsophisticated. In general, they see no advantage for themselves in freedom of speech or freedom of thought. "Those who sit in the seats of the high and mighty are selected and formed by means of power, their sources of wealth, and the mechanics of celebrity which prevail in our society," said C. Wright Mills.

Shils wrote: "William Ogburn's conception of "cultural lag" as the cause of the difficulties of modern Western societies was much like Mannheim's view that trouble is caused for a society when past and present things coexist ... *We are now witnessing an unprecedented public struggle between Christian Fundamentalists and other citizens of all religious stripes.*" They are right to be worried if Malraux was right: "If our civilization is not the first to deny the immortality of the soul, it is certainly the first for which the soul has no importance."

Religion Is The Unhealthy Denial Of Facts And Knowledge

In America, popular religion has not kept pace with technical and cultural progress in any field. Christian Fundamentalists still go along with John Calvin, who said "God, who is perfect righteousness, cannot love the iniquity which He sees in all. All of us, therefore, have that within us which deserves the hatred of God ... And therefore the very infants themselves, since they bring with them their own damnation from their mother's womb, are bound not by another's *but by their own fault.*" Today, Calvin would be regarded as a lunatic if he were an American.

Shils said "As society became more rationalized with the growth of the national state and extension of education, the secular bias of the movement of rationalization slowly and unsteadily began to reach into the culture of less educated classes." However, he said, "the progressivistic, rationalistic, emancipatory outlook is borne with strong conviction by a relatively small proportion of its proponents" (referring to well-educated people.)

Thus perhaps a majority of Americans, judging by voting patterns, still believe that our civilization depends upon *more* religion, not less. Contemporary university education is rejected by religionists because it is obviously inconsistent with religion and confuses most people. Whitehead said "I consider Christian theology to be one of the great disasters of the human race … It would be impossible to imagine anything more unChristlike than theology. Christ probably couldn't have understood it …"

Religion Is Mentally Unhealthy

"The man of belief is necessarily a dependent man … He does not belong to himself, but to the author of the idea he believes," said Nietzsche. Jim Jones said, just before the mass suicides of his brainwashed believers, "To me, death is not a fearful thing. It's living that is cursed." If that is not sick, nothing is. "If 50 million people believe a foolish thing, it is still a foolish thing," said Anatole France.

In a recent book about Christian evangelistic customs called *Fits, Trances, and Visions,* Anne Taves, a teacher of history at a theological college, wrote: "… oracular visions, sudden miracles and mass hysteria, the seance, the tent revival, the political party convention, the blues and the outdoor rock concert were classed as similar experiences. There have been thousands of cases of clearly neurotic and psychotic people, including children, who are gladly accepted as prophets and religious seers by Fundamentalist Christians and (mainly in Europe) even by Catholics. Taves considers whether such experiences come from god, the Devil or a heated imagination, whether the head or the heart produces these visions, and whether they can best be explained by hypnosis, insanity, sympathetic imitation, the Holy Spirit or just weakness of character. Many of the biggest, large-scale religious events described by historians are now believed to be examples only of mass hysteria, which is a well-documented and generally accepted phenomenon: taking leave of your senses.

According to Freud, the Oedipus complex, with its mixture of dependence, love and hostility, was seen as the key to religious symbolism. He said that religious symbolism reflects psychic conflict between father and son. "Religion is a mass obsessional neurosis ... patently infantile, ... incongruent with reality." Nathaniel Branden, author of *The Six Pillars of Self-Esteem*, wrote: "Religion is a form of escape and illness. Anyone who engages in the practice of psychotherapy confronts every day the devastation wrought by the teachings of religion." Emerson said "The theological problems of original sin, origin of evil, predestination, and the like are the soul's mumps, and measles, and whooping coughs."

Gibbon said: "The evidence of the heavenly witnesses—the Father, the Word, and the Holy Ghost—would now be rejected in any court of Justice." In fact, they are now rejected in American courts. Anne Morrow Lindbergh said "No new sect ever had humor; no disciples either, even the disciples of Christ." Nietzsche said "In individuals insanity is rare but in groups, parties, nations and epochs it is the rule ... All religions bear traces of the fact that they arose during the intellectual immaturity of the human race—before it had learned the obligations to speak the truth."

Woody Allen said "I'm going to give my psychoanalyst one more year, then I'm going to Lourdes." Lily Tomlin said "When we talk to God we're said to be praying but when God talks to us, we're schizophrenic?" Noting that religious people have few views of their own, Dr. Albert Ellis said "This kind of absolutistic, perfectionistic thinking is the prime creator of the two most corroding of human emotions: anxiety and hostility. Democracy, permissiveness, and the acceptance of human fallibility are quite alien to the real religionist." He concluded that "religiosity, to a large degree, essentially is masochism; and both are forms of mental sickness."

Mencken said: "Faith may be defined briefly as an illogical belief in the occurrence of the improbable ... A man full of faith is simply one who has lost (or never had) the capacity for clear and realistic thought. He is not a mere ass; he is actually ill." Robert Pirsig said "When a person suffers from a delusion, it is called insanity. When many people suffer from a delusion it is called religion."

"Religion is comparable to a childhood neurosis," said Freud. "Anyone who engages in the practice of psychotherapy confronts every day the devastations wrought by the teachings of religions," said Nathanial Banden. "Religion is not insanity but it is born of the stuff which makes for insanity ... all religions perform the function of delusion," said Freud. "While it cannot be proved retrospectively that any experience of possession, conversion, revelation, or divine ecstasy was merely an epileptic discharge, we must ask how one differentiates "real transcendence" from neuropathies that produce the same extreme realness, profundity, ineffability, and sense of cosmic unity," he said.

Sacrificing one's life for god by giving up human pleasures is not a noble thing: it is a waste of one's life. Personality psychologists treat people with religious behavior like that. Fasting is another time-honored support for religion. Russell said "From a scientific point of view, we can make no distinction between the man who eats little and sees heaven and the man who drinks much and sees snakes. Each is in an abnormal physical condition and therefore has abnormal perceptions." A popular joke is: "What's the difference between a preacher and psycho?" Answer: "They hear different voices in their heads."

As Long As America Has Free Speech, Religion Is Doomed

Tom Wolfe said "Today educated people look upon religions ties ... as a matter of social pedigree. It is only art that they look upon religiously." Coleridge said: "He who begins by loving Christianity better than truth, will proceed by loving his own sect or Church better than Christianity, and end in loving himself better than all."

Religious fundamentalists have become the butt of public humor among educated people. Some of the jokes are quite nasty, but they do indicate public perceptions, such as this one from Lenny Bruce: "He is a born again Christian. The trouble is, he suffered brain damage during rebirth."

Bloom's take on religion is: "Nobody is quite certain of what the religious institutions are supposed to do anymore, but they do have some kind of role either responding to a real human need or as the vestige of what was once a need, and they invite the exploitation of quacks, adventurers, cranks and fanatics."

Although Sartre was violently criticized during his lifetime, his message was not negative but positive: if you don't take responsibility for creating your own life, you are *nothing*. Even our current, dopey, illogical self-help books say that! Yet he is still criticized by Christians for *advocating "nothingness!"* It was just the opposite: he was trying to show us a way of escaping the personal nothingness of social and religious conformity.

CREATIONISM IN THE CLASSROOM

CHAPTER 6

SCIENTIFIC TRUTH

*"In the realm of science all attempts to find
any evidence of supernatural beings, of metaphysical conceptions, as God, immortality,
infinity, etc., thus far have failed, and if we are
honest we must confess that in science there
exists no God, no immortality, no soul or mind
as distinct from the body."*
—**Charles P. Steinmetz**

Steve Martin gave us a good example of how the work of
scientists appears to most of us, as follows: "The Feynman
Dilemma: A diner says to a waiter, What's this fly doing in my
soup? And the waiter says, It looks like the backstroke. Yet if
the same scene is viewed while plunging into a black hole at the
speed of light, it will look like a Mickey Mouse lunch pail from
the thirties, except that Mickey's head has been replaced by a
Lincoln penny." (From "Pure Drivel"). Feynman was one of the
builders of the first atomic bomb.

The difference between science and religion is this: In

religion, if facts don't conform to belief, they must be disposed of. In science, if facts don't conform to theory, the theory must be disposed of. That is obvious, but unfortunately science seems "wild and crazy" to most people everywhere, who think scientists are a type of "intellectual." In fact, scientists are hands-on, hard-nosed practical people, engineers and mechanics. In his best-selling book, "Surely You're Joking, Mr. Feynman," he described his career in down-to-earth terms, including lock-picking. He once stole important secret papers from the Government's files and gave them to his boss to "prove his theory" that they were not safe. He was also good at doing complex calculations in his head, including gambling odds. At a table once in Las Vegas, Jimmy the Greek said (agreeing with Feynman's theory of gambling): "I don't bet on the table; instead, I bet with people around the table who have prejudices—superstitious ideas about lucky numbers."

Scientists Deal With The Real World.

Science, not religion, deals with "the ultimate." Burbank said "Science is knowledge arranged and classified according to truth, facts, and the general laws of nature ... The god within us is the only available god we know and the clear light of science teaches us that we must be our own saviors." Ingersoll wrote: "The hope of science is the perfection of the human race." Koestler said that science was "the art of the soluble," meaning that metaphysics and religion only deal with the insoluble. Beryl Bainbridge said in reference to god: "science has got rid of him." Adam Smith said: "Science is the greatest antidote to the poison of enthusiasms and superstition." "The power of accurate observation is commonly called cynicism by those who have not got it," said Shaw. Pasteur said "Science knows no country."

Science depends on free and cooperative communication among all scientists and members of the general public. David Sarnoff, former chairman of RCA, said "Freedom is the oxygen without which science cannot breathe." Prof. Grinnell said "... scientists, like most people, assume that the world is real and has a constant underlying order ... Neither of these assumptions in itself is scientific; each is derived from the way that most people experience the world." Dawkins said "Science offers you the privilege before you die of understanding why you were ever born in the first place." Who are these men and women who have made god irrelevant, and how did they do that?

Inevitably, each type of science develops its own vocabulary, as well as its own peculiar outlook (or inlook, in the case of things that can be taken apart). Thus, errors and misunderstandings, although ever present, are kept to a minimum by constant repetition, testing, hundreds of thousands of scientific experiments and scholarly papers and, eventually, application to the real world. It is virtually impossible, therefore, to discuss "science" without a clear understanding of what different "sciences" are.

Science Has Made Religion Obsolete

Both science and religion deal with the same thing: how the world works. Science gives us answers based on everything that is discoverable; religion gives us answers based on the human imagination only. Before we can talk about scientific theory and its cultural value, however, we need to know what scientists do every day, as follows.

Astronomy

Astronomers examine that part of the universe that can be seen with optical telescopes or measured by radio-telescopes, and spend a lot of time outdoors at night far away from big cities and other sources of light. (Astrologists, on the other hand, are so ignorant of actual planets, asteroids, etc., that they think the stars in each "constellation" are near each other in some kind of pattern.) Incredibly, every year college students sign up for astronomy thinking it is "astrology"! Some don't discover their mistake until they ask the professor what "sign" he/she is.

Biology

We should keep in mind that DNA was here before humans evolved, as Dawkins said "They are in you and me; they created us, body and mind; and their preservation is the ultimate rationale for our existence ... They go by the name of genes, and *we* are *their* survival mechanism." It was a biologist who discovered that the male praying mantis cannot copulate until the female rips off its head. ("Hi honey I'm home!" she says, and he responds like this: "Oh. What? ... aaargh!") What can a scientist learn from rats, you might ask? As one lab rat said to the other lab rat, "I've got my scientist trained to feed me when I press this buzzer."

Chemistry

Chemists sing chemistry songs, such as The Uranium Song: "I Get a Kick out of You." It is said, as you might expect, that a chemist reading a book about helium (which is lighter than air) can't put it down. It is well known that people (other than chemists) think lab science is basically funny. Stephen Wright's joke goes: "I mixed this myself. Two parts H, one part O. I don't trust anybody. They say we're 98% water ... We are that close to drowning! ... I bought some powdered water, but I don't know what to add to it."

Engineering

Engineers are viewed as would-be physicists who couldn't cut it (see below). They are said to think up stuff like: "44 ways to get electric power from hamsters" (one of which is: "Go to Radio Shack and trade a hamster for two AAA batteries.") It has been said that you are engineer material if your wristwatch has more power than your laptop. They look forward to Christmas so they can assemble kids' toys.

Geology

They sing: "Geologists all bold and strong / We are the subject of this song / Where flies are thick, we never walk / They carry *us* from rock to rock."

Mathematics, Probability and Statistics

Statistics and probability are branches of mathematics, which is considered to be a science. According to Internet science buffs, "If an infinite number of rednecks riding in an infinite number of pickup trucks fire an infinite number of shotgun rounds at an infinite number of highway signs, they will eventually produce all the world's great literary works in Braille."

Physics

Einstein said, in effect "The faster you go, the shorter you are," and inspired thousands of jokes. "There was a young couple named Bright / Whose fucking was faster than light / They went at it one day in a relative way / and came back on the previous night." Here is an advanced physics question that is in fact answerable, although silly: "A large plane full of nuns and orphans weighing 150,000 pounds travelling at 724.66 mph at an altitude of 40,000 meters suffers explosive decompression above the center of a 30km diameter population. Assuming that one passenger is sucked out every 1.8 seconds, how many bodies will land within the population center?"

Another popular pastime of science students and teachers is inventing wrong conclusions that seem to make sense, but don't, about common phenomena such as light bulbs. Under the "Dark Sucker Theory," electric bulbs don't give off "light." They suck "dark" from the surroundings. Once they are full of dark, they no longer work. (This, believe it or not, is exactly how Christian Fundies explain natural phenomena, arguing that "dark" is also a "substance" created by god, according to the Bible.)

Dave Barry explained electricity experiments this way: "If you scuffed your feet long enough without touching anything you would build up so much many electrons that your finger would explode. This is nothing to worry about unless you have carpeting." Anthony Stanton explained the difference between chemistry and physics: "Chemists are, on the whole, like physicists, only less so ... They have their moments, and sources of legitimate pride. They don't split atoms like the physicists do. They join them together, and a very praiseworthy activity that is." Feynman said "Physics is like sex. Sure, it may give some practical results, but that's not why we do it."

Medicine, Psychology And Psychiatry

Why did you choose social psychology? the great Dr. Pavlov was once asked. "They always had food at their meetings," he said, indicating his early interest in making dogs salivate by ringing dinner bells (now called "behaviorism").

The Scientific Method

All scientists spend an inordinate amount of time making up fake but technical sounding "scientific rules," such as the Jennings corollary: "The chance of the bread falling with the butter side down is directly proportional to the cost of the carpet." The essence of all science is understanding how the world works and then classifying its components and categories. For example: "To err is human; to moo, bovine." It may well be that science is more accurate than religion because there are no taboos among scientists. Here is what scientists think about ordinary people: "There was once a fly on the wall / I wonder why doesn't it fall? / Because its feet stuck? / Or was it just luck? / Or does gravity just miss things so small?" In general, scientific rules are merely summaries of discoveries and not "rules" at all.

The Differences Between Science And Religion

One of the major differences between religion and science is that scientists have a sense of humor and religionists do not. In order to get the votes of the ignorant (or "scientifically challenged"), politicians say that science must be wrong because it is incompatible with the Bible. "Physics is not a religion. If it were, we'd have a much easier time raising money," said L. Lederman. In general, science is criticized because most of it does not result in any progress whatsoever. "Results! Why, man, I have gotten a lot of results. I know several thousand things that won't work," said Edison. The result of this public attitude is that science is not mandatory in many schools, on the theory first propounded by Samuel Butler: "Genius is a nuisance, and it is the duty of schools and colleges to abate it by setting genius traps in its way."

"The general public has long been divided into two parts: those who think that science can do anything, and those who are afraid that it will," said Dixy Lee Ray. Leno said: "Scientists say that your nose and ears continue to grow over the course of your lifetime. If that's the case, Evander Holyfield might want to fight Tyson again just to get a trim." Berle remarked that the reason that lightning never hits the same place twice is that, after it hits the first time, the "same place" isn't "there" anymore. The general public also has a tendency to equate scientists and science with odd-ball things like robots, as illustrated by this Berle joke: "I know a girl who thinks she's a robot because she was made by a scientist." Also, there are always wise guys who ask how does science help the business world, as if that were a real question! There are hundreds of good answers, including: "Where would the belt business be without the law of gravity?" Not to mention Bill Gates.

Pure Science vs. Lab Science

Basically, there are two kinds of science: "pure science" (also known as "thinking") and laboratory work. The lab scientists wear white lab coats and have repetitive jobs. There is an old tradition that the general public at almost any moment can vent their anger at science by attacking the nearest lab where people in white coats, like Dr. Frankenstein, are developing ungodly new kinds of machines, living organisms and deadly substances, etc. People are suspicious of science.

The difference between science and religion can also be illustrated by the following jokes: Why did the chicken cross the road? "Pure chance," say the scientists, or else: "only the fittest survive." (Hawking's theory is that everything that ever happened was programmed during the first few seconds following the Big Bang, including the proclivities of chickens.) A creationist might say: "God created the chicken on the other side of the road to start with," because, to a devout Christian, the answer to every question is "GOD."

Most science work is drudgery. A scientist named Cartmill once said: "As an adolescent I aspired to lasting fame, I craved factual certainty, and I thirsted for a meaningful vision of human life—so I became a scientist. This is like becoming an archbishop so you can meet girls." Scientists, in turn, like to poke fun at religious reasoning. "I can prove anything, given that $1+1=1$," Russell once said. "Okay, prove that you are the Pope," a friend challenged. Russell said "I am one, the Pope is one. Therefore, the Pope and I are one." Scientists and statisticians are not similar to Christians in any way, except, possibly, that they never die: "they are just broken down by age and sex."

Scientists spend a lot of their time making jokes about "Creationism." For example: "1. It is a scientifically established fact that the stork does exist. 2. Everybody knows that a baby is age zero when born, not nine months. 3. There are several well-documented cases where sexual intercourse has *not* led to the birth of a child. 5. In The Netherlands (home of the stork), both the birth rate and the number of storks are *decreasing*. 6. The theory of the stork can be investigated by rigorous scientific methods once the sex theory is abandoned." (Apologies to Prof. Aalto). Unscientific theories are nonsense.

The Scientific Method

Scientists are the only ones who can tell us correctly How the World Works in exquisite detail. For example: "The sperm of the whale known as the Black Right Whale has four kilos of brains and 1000 kilos of testicles. If it thinks at all, we know what it thinks about," said Prof. John Lien. That kind of knowledge is always subject to correction by future research, which may determine that the testicles weigh somewhat more or less. You can bet that, if scientists can know that, they must know a lot of other neat stuff that Christian Fundamentalists don't want you to know. For example, humans and dolphins are the only species that have sex for pleasure. Don't you think we might learn more about sex by studying dolphins?

The technique of science and rational thinking is never to draw any conclusions not supported by actual observation, as illustrated by this story of an engineer, an experimental physicist, a theoretical physicist, and a philosopher hiking in Scotland. When they saw a black sheep, the engineer said "The sheep in Scotland are black." The physicist said "Well, some of them are black." The theoretical physicist then says "Well, at least one of the sheep is black. Then the philosopher says "On one side, anyway." A religionist, on the other hand, might say: "Men are to sheep what god is to man," which is a meaningless Biblical statement because it says nothing about sheep, man or god (but sounds profound from a pulpit).

Naturally, what was scientifically true ten years ago is not true today. (When a student complained to Einstein that the questions on this year's test was the same as last year's, Einstein said "Yes, but the answers are different.") James Randi, who makes a living by debunking phony claims about astrology and the paranormal, etc., wrote a book about faith healers in which he offered to give one million dollars to anyone providing evidence of healing through prayer. Nobody has successfully proved any such cure. All they have to do is give a demonstration in front of a group of scientists! Michael White, in his book, *Weird Science*, explained why astrology, ghosts, voodoo, UFO's, "miracles" and other "paranormal" phenomena are false. Almost any scientific theory can be proved by appropriate tests. For example, the theory that "he that laughs last, thinks the slowest" might be shown by timed motion pictures of students in a large audience. Grad students might be selected that way.

"My goal is simple," said Hawking, who probably knows more about how the universe works than any other living person. "It is a complete understanding of the universe, why it is as it is and why it exists at all." (He also said "Scientific discovery may not be better than sex, but the satisfaction lasts longer.") "Science is an integral part of culture. It's not this foreign thing done by an arcane priesthood," said Gould. "Science has proof without any certainty, Creationists have certainty without any proof," explained Ashley Montague. *There is no struggle between science and religion because religion is not a factor at all, except in the political or emotional sense.* Hoffer wrote: "Where there is the necessary technical skill to move mountains, there is no need for faith to move mountains." Shils wrote: "Since the postulate of the search for knowledge defines the task of the scientist as the "falsification" of what has been received, only through the process of continuous falsification of prior beliefs does science progress ... Doubt being the beginning of scientific activity, only that which survives the test of contemporary doubt can be accepted as valid scientific knowledge." Renan wrote: "No miracle has ever taken place under conditions which science can accept."

The Role Of Probability

Scientists do not postpone their conclusions until they have all possible data because, if they didn't, we'd still be waiting for the atomic bomb to be built. What happens in science is that probabilities are good enough for making conclusions because usually, that is all there is. "Errors using inadequate data are much less than those using no data at all," said Babbage. Data is then analyzed by experiments. (In fact, experimenting with life is what all smart men and women do, in order to understand it.) Scientists try to avoid jumping to conclusions if additional experiments can still be done. A scientific rule is good if it cannot be "falsified" by investigation. That approach does not work with religion because it is already false, and cannot be confirmed. (Gravity: "not just a good idea—it's the law!)

Why don't religionists take the same approach to religious laws to strengthen their arguments? A new religious "rule" might be, for example: "Psychic forces are sufficient in most human bodies for a shock or a revelation to propel them rapturously away from the earth's surface to heaven, fully clothed." The "data" supporting that conclusion would have to consist of Biblical quotations, which would substitute for facts. Or, "the amount of pure adoration of god in a church service is determined by multiplying the number of worshippers by the number of cubic feet of space in the church and dividing by the volume of singing and other human sound, and subtracting the number of people not singing or wailing." Whitehead said: "When a religious belief is proved wrong, it is accepted as a defeat for religion; but when a scientific proposition is proved wrong, it is a triumph for science."

Unlike politicians and preachers, scientists never announce conclusions of fact that are still open to questions of any kind. For example, they don't just say that Santa Claus could not possibly use reindeer to deliver presents; they first make calculations. For example: "No known species of reindeer can fly. But there are 300,000 living organisms yet to be classified. And, while most of these are insects and germs, this does not completely rule out flying reindeer, which only Santa has ever seen." As for Santa himself: "He will be subjected to centrifugal forces 17,500.06 times greater than gravity. A 250-pound Santa ... would be pinned to the back of his sleigh by 4,315 pounds of force." [thanks to Alexander Associates]. The opposite of scientific law is Gell-Mann's Law, which is used as a proof of god's existence by silly religionists: "Whatever isn't forbidden is required; thus, if there's no reason why something shouldn't exist, then it must exist." At some point, of course, further thinking will be a waste of time. Most Christians say "god gave us brains, so let's use them," which creates a dilemma: "if we use them, god makes no sense." To avoid that, they think: "god did not give us brains to deny god," so (with god's approval) we must not question god's existence. Thus, a Christian idea of using your brain is to use it only for certain approved purposes, meaning that, most of the time, their brains are turned off.

John Hunter joked: "Why think? Let's try the experiment." Roentgen also said "I didn't think; I experimented." That can be understood two ways: If you don't think first, the experiment will not think for you. But after you have thought of everything you can, it must be tested. "A fool ... is a man who never tried an experiment in his life," said Charles Darwin's grandfather. One method of measuring change or other quality is to use one specimen for experiment and another as a "control" to gauge the difference at the end of the experiment. Scientists joke that, when a biologist has twins, he baptizes one and keeps the other for a "control specimen" (which would be interesting if one were sent to a religious school and the other to a public school; based on college entrance tests, the baptized one would learn the least.) Thus, making mistakes can be good!

To a scientist, that is progress because each mistake brings him closer to what is really going on. (To a religionist, making thousands of mistakes shows how futile and useless science is.)

Intuition is another key ingredient in scientific work. "It is through science that we prove, but through intuition that we discover," said Poincaré. Also, many discoveries are made by chance and error. A well-known maxim of science is: "Discoveries are made by not following instructions." Science takes time, usually an amount of time not known in advance. "Crash programs fail because they are like the theory that, with nine women pregnant, you can get a baby in a month," joked von Braun.

Buckminster Fuller said "Now there is one outstandingly important fact regarding Spaceship Earth, and that is that no instruction booklet comes with it." Scientists know that there is no master plan for the evolution of the universe and everything in it, and that, if events on earth had happened just a bit differently, the results would have been different, too. Pascal said "Had Cleopatra's nose been shorter, the whole face of the world would have been different," meaning that, with a less pretty nose, Cleopatra would not have been able to seduce Anthony, etc. "The true men of action in our time, those who transform the world, are not the politicians and the statesmen, but the scientists," said the poet W. H. Auden. "Unfortunately, poetry cannot celebrate them because their deeds are concerned with things, not persons, and are, therefore, speechless. When I find myself in the company of scientists, I feel like a shabby curate who has strayed by mistake into a drawing room full of dukes." Bulwer-Lytton said "In science, read by preference the newest works; in literature, the oldest." "A man's mind stretched by a new idea can never go back to its original dimensions," said Oliver Wendell Holmes Jr. "The truth wars longer than all the gods; for it is only in the truth's service, and for love of it, that people have overthrown the gods and at last God himself," said Max Stirner.

Science Is Concerned With Facts and Data

It is the business of science to establish what is a "fact," to the extent possible. Joseph Campbell, by referring to the work of scientists, has pointed out that the supposedly true and meaningful story of Christ's birth is basically a copy of an even earlier myth, as follows: "The night of December 25, to which date the Nativity of Christ was ultimately assigned, was exactly that of the birth of the Persian savior Mithra, who, as an incarnation of eternal light, was born the night of the winter solstice (then dated December 25) at midnight, the instant of the turn of the year from increasing darkness to light." That information constitutes "real knowledge" about the origin of Christianity. We can't blame Christ's apostles for adopting that myth because it is not likely they actually knew about it. Scientists are pragmatic, and accept whatever seems to work. Thus if something works, accept it and then try to figure out why; it would be foolish to ignore a fact just because you can't yet explain *how* it works. "Reasoning draws a conclusion—but does not make the conclusion certain, unless the mind discovers it by the path of experience," wrote Bacon. Newton, long before his time, also saw the futility of purely intellectual reasoning: "Physics! Preserve me from metaphysics!" Edison said: "The hope of theology is the salvation of the few and the damnation of almost everybody." Also he said "I have never seen the slightest scientific proof of the religious theories of heaven and hell, of eternal life for individuals, or of a personal God." "We ... live on an insignificant planet of a humdrum star lost in a galaxy tucked away in some forgotten corner of a universe in which there are far more galaxies than people," said Sagan. Von Braun summed things up this way, based only on what can be known so far: "We are all on a spaceship, and that spaceship is Earth. Four billion passengers—and no skipper."

"The most beautiful thing we can experience is the mysterious. It is the source of all true art and science," said

Einstein. "As long as men are free to ask what they must—free to say what they think—free to think what they will—freedom can never be lost and science can never regress," said Oppenheimer. "Knowledge for the sake of understanding, not merely to prevail, that is the essence of our being," said Vannevar Bush. "Science is the greatest antidote to the poison of enthusiasm and superstition," said Adam Smith.

By way of contrast, the supreme religious leader of Saudi Arabia said, in 1993 "The earth is flat. Whosoever claims it is round is an atheist deserving of punishment" (proving once again that religious knowledge is not knowledge). "Truth does not demand belief" said somebody very smart. "Scientists do not join hands every Sunday, singing, "Yes, gravity is real! I will have faith! I will be strong!"

How Do Scientists "Know" Something?"

"Every great advance in natural knowledge has involved the absolute rejection of authority," said T. H. Huxley. Hannah Arendt said: "What science and the quest for knowledge are after is *irrefutable* truth; that is, propositions that human beings are not free to reject—*that are compelling*. They are two kinds, as we have known since Leibnitz: truths of reasoning and truths of fact." Science is nothing more than understanding the world we live in, i.e., "reality." As Bronowski explained in "The Ascent of Man," primitive man survived by applying science, or trial and error, in order to find out what works and what does not work. *Tools were all developed by experimentation*. Primitive man, like modern man, made his own discoveries; god did not tell him how to make fire, an ax, a wheel or a bow-lathe. Many tribes never discovered how to make fire, and became extinct. Some of the first scientists became priests of their tribes because they were able to predict things like the phases of the moon, and the rising of the stars in their constellations. *Here we are today in the year 2003, and religious peo-*

ple are outraged at the thought that scientists can take the place of priests!

Science searches the world by putting as much light as possible on it; religion works by closing our eyes to reality in order to better imagine the invisible. "Science is the search for truth—it is not a game in which one tries to beat his opponent, to do harm to others," said Pauling. Anatole France said "Nature has no principles. She makes no distinction between good and evil." Arthur Lornberg, a Nobel laureate, said "A scientist … shouldn't be asked to judge the economic and moral value of his work. All we should ask the scientist to do is find the truth—and then not keep it from anyone." Oppenheimer said: "There must be no barriers to freedom of inquiry. There is no place for dogma in science. The scientist must be free to ask any question, to doubt any assertion, to seek for any evidence, to correct any errors."

The Big Breakthrough: How Do We "Know" Anything?

Robert Graves, the British novelist and classical scholar, said "… no scientist, however specialized his field, can factually accept even the book of Genesis; and what the scientist thinks today, everyone else will be thinking on the day after tomorrow." Jacques Monod, a leading contemporary philosopher, said "Unlike religion, the scientific attitude implies … that there is no plan; that there is no intention in the universe." *Since there is no God's plan, people must, with the help of science, make their own plan.*

The "scientific method" is the work product of a number of modern thinkers, including Comte, Condorcet, Hume and Mill. Comte two centuries ago described three successive methods of explaining the world: (1) theological, in terms of the will of the gods; (2) metaphysical, in terms of purely philosophical abstraction and imagination; and (3) "positive," in terms of specific scientific knowledge. Today, "positivism" rules. Positivism does not mean that we can be "positive" we are correct; it means only that we must deal only with "positive"—that is—"real" things, as distinct from imaginary things. The word "theory," as used by scientists, means "plausible explanation," not "wild and crazy guess."

In the *Dictionary of the History of Ideas* (Charles Scribner's Sons, 1973) an article edited by Shirley Brown Letwin summarized this matter substantially as follows. "Condorcet said that there is no essential difference between the natural and social sciences because all laws about experience are not more than probable anyway. Mill adopted this attitude and proposed that the key to correct thinking lay in logic: "… the laws of the investigation of truth by means of extrinsic evidence whether rationative or inductive …" He said that induction was a sound method and showed that scientific truth was unquestionably "valid" even if not demonstrably "certain." *In other words, we have to start with the most reasonable, most easily believable idea that can't be refuted and build on that.* If it makes sense to you and me, then it is valid as a starting point. Only religion has absolute knowledge.

Two "common sense philosophers"—Englishmen Reid and Beattie—argued in the 19th century that knowledge was based on self-evident truths which, though impossible to prove, are also impossible to disbelieve, making them valid starting points. Reid said there was an intuitive first principle, "an instantaneous and instinctive impulse, acting independently of our will, whenever its object is present … called Sense: and acting in a similar manner upon all mankind, and therefore properly called Common Sense." In other words, we have to start somewhere; we can't refuse to believe anything just because we can't prove everything.

Almost without public notice, a way of thinking about, and actually defining, "reality" was discovered in the 20th century. Few people ever heard about it, and most people today still think that "reality" is purely personal and speculative, so that one man's reality is as good as another's. Americans confuse their *right* to believe whatever they want with the question whether anything at all can be "known." It is common today for people to say things like "everything is a matter of opinion." While this is better than saying "my religion is absolutely true," it is still no good. *The fact is, as modern philosophers know, it is not only possible but necessary to discover "facts" that are not figments of imagination.* Who were the geniuses that proved this astonishing thing? Unfortunately, public schools cannot teach these things because religionists continue to say all scientific ideas are "controversial" (as if religion isn't!). Hold on to your hats, folks, because the truth is out!

It was G.E. Moore and Russell who provided the foundation of modern scientific philosophy and explained the futility of trying to account for anything spiritual in science. *They wrote that truth consisted in the correspondence of thought to the external world, and nothing more.* (Their names should be familiar to every high school kid but, unfortunately, they are not even familiar to most high school teachers.) Thus, truth is not something good or noble or spiritual, but whatever is the way things actually are. Moore, for example, said there were many things that could not reasonably be doubted; for example, that he was a person with two hands, speaking to others.

Russell seems to be the first who required that the ground for certainty be totally independent of human beings. From that point, Russell based his system only on ideas that could be rationally defended, whether they were perfect proofs or not, and whether they fully explained any overall general principle or not. In effect, he said: let's start with what we do know, whether it is complete or incomplete. (In earlier times, philosophers felt compelled to write nothing unless they could explain everything by their theory! That is why all the late Renaissance philosophers make no sense to us now.)

Russell began by analyzing common sense beliefs to discover whether there was "any knowledge in the world which is so certain that no reasonable man could doubt it." He found that although we can question the existence of material objects such as "a table," that we think we are looking at, we cannot doubt the existence of the "sense data" which made us think there was a table there. *In other words, the table can't be entirely a figment of my imagination if the man next to me describes the same thing I think I see.* If we each describe the same "sense data," that is the equivalent of saying that the data actually relates to *something that cannot be denied.*

The first step, therefore, is to record and measure the data that we can quantify or explain even partially—for example, "Whatever else may be doubtful, some at least of our immediate experiences seem absolutely certain." If 1,000 sane people each examined a certain table and measured it and described it in exactly the same way, then a scientist is justified in saying that there is such a thing as a table having those specific qualities (which is what judges in our courts do every day). Theoretically, this method could be applied to religious phenomena that could be measured in some way, or which constantly recurred based upon scientific data. Since we cannot describe or measure god, or angels, or a spiritual world, it is not possible for rational people to talk about such "things" in any coherent or useful manner.

The Test That All Rational People Can Agree On

Thus Moore and Russell concluded there must be an "external world" out there, independent of our personal experience, that could be perceived as "facts" by everyone, based upon observation, testing and analysis. Even if what we are measuring or testing is unknown in its entirely, it is a beginning. Truth, according to Moore and Russell, consisted in the correspondence of thought to the external world (or that part of it that we can detect). That is, we have to accept whatever it was that our senses discovered, and not impose human categories on unknown phenomena. In "Ludwig Wittgenstein," by Ray Monk, the author wrote: "In fact, nothing is more *conservative* than science. Science lays down railway track. And for scientists it is important that their work should move along those tracks." Science is bound by the track, meaning the evidence and the limitations that in fact exist.

Russell and Wittgenstein also required that the ground for certainty in anything be totally independent of human beings, meaning that "things" or "data" that exist only in our brains cannot be validated. *That is, they were committed to the belief that our perception of objects that manifest themselves to us is the ultimate ground of knowledge, not some purely theoretical or metaphysical assumption or general principle of life, etc. that we can only imagine.* (If we wait for a complete explanation of everything we will wait forever and in the meantime nobody can say he really knows anything!) Russell believed in a science that is "at no moment quite right but it is seldom quite wrong ... It is, therefore, rational to accept it hypothetically" as a starting point. He noted that our educated guesses (inductive inferences) "are not disproved when what they show to be probable does not happen." He concluded that we cannot give an account of the whole reality, but only of its "structure," meaning a recurring pattern of relations in time and space among events we perceive (whose causes or subjects are unknown.) He showed that science could achieve definite answers and successive approximations to the truth in which each new stage results from an improvement but not a rejection of what had gone before. Thus all a scientist can do is to reduce the risk of error that is always present.

In effect, scientists gradually discover what the object is *not*, rather than what it *is*. That, of course, is far more accurate than any pure (religious) speculation could ever be. Unscientific explanations for events are successively replaced by scientific explanations, which are ever closer approximations to the final answer ("truth") as a "thing," or concept. Without the concept that was later discovered, the earlier events could not be explained. For example, over your neighbor's fence you might see a woman's body appearing high in the air and then dropping down behind it, over and over again every time Helen Reddy's "I Am A Woman" is being played next door. At first, speculation as to what is going on must take in everything you see and hear. You have to ask: how can that kind of music (or, logically, any kind of music) influence that body flying in the air? However, if you were a scientist you could eventually deduce that she has a trampoline behind the fence, and that *Helen Reddy's song has nothing to do with it* (according to Paula Poundstone, a scientific comedian). Any "theory" that music influenced the body's flight would be discarded.

The work of Russell and Moore was carried further by Wittgenstein and by scientists, including Heisenberg, who concluded that "reality" is not just what we actually see and measure but our own thoughts that are relevant to the reality we see. For example, Heisenberg explained that the world we are discovering by research also includes the elements added by our imagination if the idea, as so modified, still makes sense. Eventually, said he, the pieces that our imagination adds to our data will eventually be proved to exist, or, if not, the theory will be abandoned and we start over with our reasoning. This is known by the unfortunate term, "uncertainty principle," which has provided jokesters with thousands of laughs ever since.

If "Spirituality" Cannot Be Detected Or Measured, It's Not There

Thus, in order to be irrefutable, a fact, thing, phenomenon or theory need not be complete or *meaningful*, as long as it is *constant*. There can be no irrefutable truth about the whole universe, but only about parts of it that can be examined. As of the date of this book, no evidence of "spirituality" has been found by scientists, and no phenomenon discovered is in any way dependent on spirituality. That being so, you can't blame scientists for not being "spiritual" or for not discussing "spirituality."

Science Is Superior To Religion Because It Conforms To Reality

What makes science so unassailable? Russell and Wittgenstein concluded that there was no "mistake-proof" method for building up knowledge. Falsifiability, therefore, is the difference between science and nonscience. "It is ... an essential mark of a scientific hypothesis that it should be in principle falsifiable," said Karl Popper, "that there should be intelligibly describable phenomena which, if they were to happen, would by their actual occurrence show that the hypothesis was false. *Every scientific statement remains tentative forever,*" he said. "But no matter how many confirming examples you produce, it is impossible to prove the open, universal proposition with decisive finality ... No open universal proposition can ever be confirmed beyond all conceivable future correction, although some can be decisively and finally disproved." According to Whitehead, "when a religious belief is proved wrong, it is accepted as a defeat for religion; but when a scientific proposition is proved wrong, it is a triumph for science."

Popper said "Our civilization ... has not yet fully recovered from the shock of its birth—the transition from the tribal or closed society, with its submission to magical forces, to the "open society" which sets free the critical powers of man."

CHAPTER 7

RATIONALISM

"How will the truth be realized? What, in short, is the truth's cash-value in experimental terms? The moment pragmatism asks this question, it sees the answer: True ideas are those that we can assimilate, validate, corroborate, and verify. False ideas are those that we cannot. That is the practical difference it makes to us to have true ideas; that therefore is the meaning of truth, for it is all that truth is known as."

—William James

A. J. Ayer was a twentieth-century British teacher of logic who held that, in order for a statement to be meaningful, it must be *verifiable* either by sense experience or by the rules governing language usage. Ayer, together with Wittgenstein, is generally credited with putting an end to "traditional philosophy," meaning imaginative, metaphysical speculation about reality, purpose, spirit, etc. While that seems to be nothing very profound, it had the effect of ruling out words like "god," "meaning," "purpose," "right," "wrong," "grace," "heaven," "hell," "spirit," etc., because none of those words refers to something that can be accurately-defined, measured, detected, or proved to exist *outside of our conversation*. In effect Ayer said: philosophy and religion are devoid of meaning unless they refer to the real world or parts of the real world that are the same for all people.

According to a biography of Ayer in *A Life*, by Ben Rogers, he once had an encounter with Mike Tyson at a part when the model Naomi Campbell ran screaming out of a bedroom occupied by Tyson. According to accounts of the event, Tyson said to Ayer "Do you know who I am? I'm the heavyweight champion of the world." Ayer replied "And I am the former Wykeham professor of logic. We are both pre-eminent in our fields. I suggest that we talk about this like rational men." During the rational conversation that followed, Naomi Campbell rationally slipped away.

Full-time thinking, of course, is not required, or even healthy, for a balanced life. As Woody Allen said, "My brain is my second favorite organ." In the light of the wisdom of Ayer, Wittgenstein and Allen, most of the philosophical confusion about reality disappears. If you apply rationality to religion, you will no longer be religious. Socrates said: "There is only one good—knowledge; and only one evil—ignorance." Rational thinking has been around since Aristotle, the medical writers of the Hellenistic period and the Stoic school. Aristotle said "Since only humans are capable of reasoning, reason is therefore the highest of men's faculties." He also said that knowledge is, among other things, *an opinion* or a *belief with* a ra*tional explanation, thereby ruling* out *religious knowledge.*

According to the principle of rational thinking first proposed by William of Ockham in the thirteenth century, the answer with the fewest unproved assumptions is the best. A German pastor named Meister Eckhart wrote: *"What is truth?*

Truth is something so noble that if God could turn aside from it, I would keep to the truth and let God go." Paracelsus, a fifteenth century German physician, wrote, way ahead of his time: "… thoughts are free and are subject to no rule. On them rests the freedom of man, and they tower above the light of nature … create a new heaven, a new firmament, a new source of energy from which new arts flow."

About five hundred years later, Mencken said "The truth is that every priest who really understands the nature of his business is well aware that science is its natural and implacable enemy … The truth is that Christian theology, like every other theology, is not only opposed to the scientific spirit, it is also opposed to all attempts at rational thinking …"

Martin Luther said the same thing: "Reason is the greatest enemy that faith has; it never comes to the aid of spiritual things, but—more frequently than not—struggles against the divine Word, treating with contempt all that emanates from God." He also said, a little more pungently, "Reason is a whore." Francis Bacon explained the difference between rationalism and religion as follows: "If we begin with certainties, we shall end in doubts; but if we begin with doubts, and are patient in them, we shall end in certainties." Hobbes (sounding much like Wittgenstein centuries later) wrote: "True and False are attributes of speech, not things. And when speech is not, there is neither Truth nor Falsehood," meaning that human beings decide for themselves what truth is.

Spinoza wrote: "There is no rational life, therefore, without intelligence, and things are good only in so far as they assist men to enjoy that life of the mind which is determined by intelligence. Those things alone, on the other hand, we call evil which hinder man from perfecting his reason and enjoying a rational life." He also observed that "Reason, however sound, has little weight with ordinary theologians." Voltaire wrote: "The true triumph of reason is that it enables us to get along with those who do not possess it." He also wrote: "Superstition sets the whole world in flames; philosophy squelches them."

Kant wrote: "The death of dogma is the birth of reality." He also said "All our knowledge begins with the senses, proceeds then to the understanding, and ends with reason. There is nothing higher than reason." He also said: "Pure logic contains the absolutely necessary rules of thought without which there can be no ... understanding, as opposed to sense impressions and even examination of objects."

Comte wrote: "All good intellects have repeated since Bacon's time, that there can be no real knowledge but that which is based on observed facts ... It is time to complete the vast intellectual operation begun by Bacon, Descartes, and Galileo, by constructing the system of general ideas which must henceforth prevail among the human race." More recently, Dewey said "The aim of education should be to teach the child to think, not what to think." Education itself was described by H. G. Wells as "A race against catastrophe." Hugo said "A stand can be made against invasion by an army; no stand can be made against invasion by an idea." Oliver Wendell Holmes Jr. wrote: "When men have realized that time has upset many fighting faiths, they may come to believe even more than they believe the very foundations of their own conduct, that the ultimate good desired is better reached by free trade in ideas—*that the best test of truth is the power of the thought* to *get itself accepted in the competition of the market,* and truth is the only ground upon which their wishes safely can be carried out. That at any rate is the theory of our Constitution."

Shaw defined "education" as: "A succession of eye-openers each involving the repudiation of some previously held belief." Sir Julian Huxley has written that the overall process of evolution from cosmic star-dust to human society is continuous and that initially the universe was devoid of purpose. "With the appearance of homo sapiens, however, man has become the sole agent of 'purpose' and of evolutionary advance," he said. "The world itself has no "purpose," but the human race can have its own purpose." Henry Ford said "Thinking is the hardest work there is, which is probably the reason why so few engage in it." He also said: "What we call evil is simply ignorance, bumping its head in the dark." Edison said "It is astonishing what an effort it seems to be for many people to put their brains definitely and systematically to work." Russell agreed with that, but was somewhat sympathetic, as follows: "There is no effort, to my mind, that is so taxing to the individual as to think, to analyze fundamentally." Brandeis said "Many people would sooner die than think—in fact, they do so." Arnold Toynbee said "Civilization is a movement and not a condition, a voyage and not a harbor." "Wisdom comes by disillusionment," said Santayana.

While philosophers seem never to agree about how to discover anything called "absolute truth," they seem to be in general agreement that religious belief is not a form of knowledge. "So far as I can remember, there is not one word in the Gospels in praise of intelligence," said Russell. Weber said that the fundamental issue is the relation between reason (science) and the human good. The idea of change and "progress" is as American as apple pie. "The world hates change, yet it is the only thing that has brought progress," said C.F. Kettering, the man who invented the automobile self-starter. "You're either part of the solution or you're part of the problem," said Eldridge Cleaver.

Prof. Bloom wrote: "To a certain extent, our universities take the place of religion in America, in the sense that they are independent and not directly involved in political concerns; in other words, they are supposed to provide refuge to thinkers and "knowers" in good times and bad, no matter what party is in power and which ideas are popular, which is why they must remain free of politics and business … It is necessary that there be an unpopular institution in our midst that sets clarity above well being or compassion, that resists our powerful urges and temptations, that is free of all snobbism but has standards ... The essence of philosophy is the abandonment of all authority in favor of individual human reason." That is why school curriculums cannot properly be established by a majority vote of taxpayers or parents.

Logic Rules!

Today, the scientific approach to reasoning and problem-solving is applied to all aspects of life. Russell said that "every philosophical problem ... is found either to be not really philosophical at all, or else to be ... logical." Another modern philosopher, W. Van Orman Quine, wrote that logic is a science and "like any science, has as its business the pursuit of truth." Thus, in modern times, "truth" is not the province of religion but the goal of science and philosophy, and has to be discovered, tested and proved. "How often have I said to you that when you have eliminated the impossible, whatever remains, however improbable, must be the truth," said Sherlock Holmes (Arthur Conan Doyle) to Dr. Watson.

Rudolf Carnap, a leading twentieth century German-American thinker, said "Logic is no longer merely one philosophical discipline among others, but we are able to say outright: logic is the method of philosophizing." Similarly, he wrote: "Before the inexorable judgment of the new logic, all philosophy in the old sense, whether it is connected with Plato, Thomas Aquinas, Kant, Schelling or Hegel, whether it constructs a new "metaphysics of Being," or a "philosophy of spirit," proves itself to be not merely materially false, as earlier critics maintained, but logically untenable and therefore meaningless." Rationalism has tremendous momentum, which can only be stopped by a national campaign of deliberate ignorance (which has already begun in the Congress, led by Tom DeLay).

Is There Such A Thing As Non-Scientific Truth?

"Positivism" is knowledge based only upon natural phenomena as verified by science. It began in France with the great Enclyclopedia of d'Alembert and Diderot which catalogued all "knowledge," as distinct from the theological suppositions that had passed for knowledge until then. Carnap said that metaphysics is impossible because it lies beyond experience and is not "experienceable," such as, for example, "the Absolute," or the "thing in itself" lying behind actual experience, or the "essence" or "meaning" of objects or events.

William van Orman Quine, a leading contemporary logician and philosopher, wrote: "A fundamental way of deciding whether a statement is true is by comparing it, in some sense or other, with the world, or, which is the nearest we can come, by comparing it with our experience of the world." Here is an explanation of logical positivism (by a non-positivist) as set forth in a typical philosophy textbook used in recent years: "Statements that are not based on experience or that cannot be verified are regarded as nonsensical or as having some noncognitive function. All the genuine data of experience ... are the province of some special science. *Philosophy properly deals with language in other words, once the philosopher has decided that a statement is meaningful and makes some claim about the world and not merely about the way we use words, it is up to the scientist to verify the statement ... metaphysics and speculative philosophy are repudiated.*" Knowledge, not "truth," is the only rational goal of humans. "To understand all makes one tolerant," said de Stael.

Only Rational Thinking Relates To Reality

Logical thinking, then, produces truths of reasoning in everyday life the same way that it produces truths of fact in the field of science. All irrational beliefs are in another category: ideas that have no basis in reality because they cannot be tested, proved or even examined. (Unfortunately, they can be debated by unlearned people.) It makes no sense to think that there is more than one rational way of thinking, or more than one "reality" to be experienced. *"Reality" is whatever two or more people can see, measure or otherwise experience at the same time.*

In *The Power of Logical Thinking,* by Marilyn Vos Savant, she wrote: "We humans tend to believe what we're told unless we take the trouble to find out otherwise, and few of us have the inclination, the time, or even the means to accomplish such an investigation. This is one of the most serious weaknesses inherent in a democracy that values one man (or woman), one vote." (Vos Savant writes the "Ask Marilyn" column for *Parade,* the Sunday magazine supplement, and is a well-known authority on mathematical problems and gambling odds.)

The Rules For Logical Thinking

"Okay!" you say. "I'm not against it! But my school didn't have classes in logical thinking." The best textbook I could find in the public library is "Practical Logic" by Douglas J. Soccio and Vincent E. Barry. The authors said: "We need a middle position that allows us to receive the sensible and reject the nonsensical. We need to sift and filter the "input" that bombards us daily. We must so refine our powers of perception and judgment that we can distinguish the legitimate claim from the bogus ... One way to meet this need is through the study of logic and critical thinking. *Logic is the study of the rules of correct argument, and critical thinking is the careful assessment of both logical and nonlogical claims.* "

In logic, an "argument" is any group of propositions, one of which follows logically from the others. The hard drive of our brains has everything we need to think clearly, but they have not been programmed properly through education. "All our dignity lies in thought," said Pascal. "Let us strive, then, to think well." Since thinking ability is what separates humans from other mammals, we should try to be good at it. *Logic is the only form of "common language" that can unify people.* The following material also includes ideas set forth in Vos Savant's book and in *How to Think Straight*, by Flew.

The tool of logic is already used by our military services, by our most advanced technological enterprises, and by detectives. For example, if a man is observed opening a car door for a woman, a private detective could rationally deduce that either the car is new or the wife is new. Inductive logic, as distinct from deductive logic, is not itself *proof* of anything, but it is a tool that helps us solve a problem or analyze a factual situation, and is therefore "reasonable," or "probable" for a scientist or a detective to follow that assumption until it is proved right or wrong. It can be irrational to reject an idea or proposition on the ground that the outcome is not 100% certain, especially if 100% certainty is not required in order to make a decision. The closer to the truth, the better.

It may take another generation for all this to be taught in our public schools (which are very backward in the area of thinking and reasoning), but in the meantime you can bet your booty that people with an old-fashioned education will use every means available to *defeat the forces of rationality.* Jung wrote: *"The pendulum of the mind oscillates between sense and nonsense, not between right and wrong,"* meaning the issue is always logic, not religion and morality. There are text-books on how to think, just as there are textbooks on geography, football, carpentry and cooking, but few people read them because thinking is hard work. Most of the problems that exist in business, politics and technology are caused by poor thinking and the effect of emotions. "The degree of one's emotion varies inversely with one's knowledge of the facts—the less you know, the hotter you get," said Russell. Gladstone said "Men are apt to mistake the strength of their feeling for the strength of their argument. The heated mind resents the chill touch and relentless scrutiny of logic." William G. McAdoo said "It is impossible to defeat an ignorant man in an argument."

As in the case of science, logic involves what are called "arguments," which attempt to bring "evidence" in support of a "conclusion." The starting point, in all cases, is to be sure two opposing arguments are stated in plain English. As Flew has pointed out, Humpty Dumpty (in *Through the Lookingglass*) said "When I use a word, it means just what I choose it to mean" (thereby making rational conversation impossible). Ayer, Carnap, Quine and other modern philosophers take the position that no sentence can be true unless both sides understand the concept in exactly the same way. Lawyers use this method in drafting long and complex contracts, defining what precisely is meant by things like "default," "profit," "loss," "inventory," "employee," "breach," "invention," "good will," etc., so that lawsuits over "meaning" will not result from their contracts. If it ever gets to court, the most logical statements will always win.

For example, the following sentence makes no sense unless we can define the term "head of lettuce" to mean the head of the lettuce department in a supermarket: "A head of lettuce knows more than the owner of the refrigerator because he knows whether or not that light really does go out when the refrigerator door shuts." Is there any rational basis for concluding that a woman who wears her wedding ring on the "wrong finger" married "the wrong man"? Is it reasonable to deduce that, for every set of horse shoes that is found, there is a barefoot horse? Words can be used logically or illogically. Matthew Arnold, a pessimist, said "The mass of mankind will never have any ardent zeal for seeing things as they are." The function of optimists is to prove him wrong by teaching logic in schools. "There are two kinds of arguments," said Plato, "the true and the false. The young should be instructed in both—but the false first ..."

Rules Of Logical Thinking

The study of logic is based upon the concept of an "argument," meaning any group of propositions, one of which follows logically from the others. There must first be a statement of the idea to be argued, called a "premise," that is regarded as true by both sides. The premises of arguments are those statements that are claimed to support the conclusion. The conclusion is the statement that we are trying to prove is true by the process of deduction. An argument is said to be cogent if there is known good evidence for all of its premises and no known evidence against them. *The test is: Would a disinterested, rational person possessing relevant knowledge and expertise accept these premises as true? If the answer is yes, the premises are reasonable.* That is followed by the argument being made by one of the parties. For example:

1. All diamonds will scratch glass (as both sides agree).
2. The stone in Jean's ring will not scratch glass.
3. Therefore, the stone in Jean's ring is not a diamond (and her husband is *probably* going to be very unhappy).

If the premise is true to start with, and the argument is not supported by the premise, the argument fails. You will soon realize that if the premise is false, then the answer will also be false. The most common "god argument" begins with the false premise that "some power" had to create the universe. That is false because (a) it is equally possible that the universe always existed and (b) it does not answer the question because it fails to explain where god came from or how we know god exists. Also, in recent decades, scientists have determined that matter can not be exnihilated or annihilated, but always exists.

While the process of deduction is one of the tests of knowledge, it is limited to situations in which a given question is determined to be either true or false. For example, little brother remarks to little sister upstairs:

"Mom and Dad have company downstairs."

"How do you know that?"

"I heard Mom laughing at Dad's old jokes."

Another example of rational thinking (deduction) is this: "Show me a man with his head held high, and I'll show you a man with brand new bifocals." However, deduction is not always a one-stage thing; one good deduction can follow a bad one. "You need glasses," said the optician. "I am wearing glasses," said the customer. "In that case I need glasses." Here's another logical deduction: "What does it mean if I get sparks out of my knife and fork?" It probably means that you're eating too fast. Rule One is: Never overlook the simplest answer. For example: What did Paul Revere say at the end of his famous ride? Logically, you can't go wrong with "Whoa."

Here is a common type of argument:

"Anyone who buys hamburgers at Joe's is a fool."

"Sam is no fool."

"Therefore, Sam does not buy hamburgers at Joe's."

That is a bad argument because the unspoken premise implies something that it does not say—that the food there is no good. Here is another implied premise: "My three-year-old is so advanced he can spell his name backwards," says Joe. "So can mine, and he's only two," says Bill, which proves nothing if the kid's name is Otto. Here's another example:

"All churchgoers are patriotic.

Jones is patriotic.

Therefore Jones must be a churchgoer."

(The premise may be false also: all churchgoers may not be patriotic.) Note that an argument can be logical in theory but false as applied to a particular person. For example:

All religious people are good people.

Entwhistle is a good person.

Therefore, Entwhistle is religious.

It is possible that, in fact, Entwhistle is a good person who is not religious. Another problem with the argument is that the first statement is not provable and probably false by itself. If you can't see that, you may be just a sucker.

Here's another: "All Christians believe in an omnipotent and personal god, and Mother Mabel believed in an omnipotent and personal god. Therefore Mother Mabel was a Christian." It is possible—on the basis of only the above statement—that Mother Mabel was a Jew or a Hindu. Here's another, more difficult one: "I knew he was cheating on me with his secretary because the lipstick on his collar was covered with "Wite-Out" paint." He probably was. Deduction: If a person uses a grocery cart in the 7-Eleven, that person must have bad eating habits. Here's another: It may be logical to think that, if real trains have train schedules, toy trains must have toy train schedules, but what is logical can also be wrong (or absurd besides!).

The Need For Authorities, Experts And Proofs

There is a joke about one French Impressionist painter, Manet or Corot perhaps, who tells another that the chicken in one of his paintings was painted wrong: "That is not how a chicken's leg goes!" he tells him. The other painter replies: "In my opinion, sir, that is how a chicken's leg goes." Neither of them, evidently, thought of checking out chicken anatomy at the local library, museum, or butcher. For almost everyone, therefore, there must be reliance upon "authority" for what exists and what does not exist, and for how the world works, meaning not a single person as a guru, but the collective knowledge of many educated people set down in writing. Obviously, a guru sitting in a cave cannot be an authority in the field of atomic structure or marital tensions, although he may be an authority for the psychological stress of living alone. Encyclopedias are good authorities for the simple reason that hundreds of scholars must cooperate to produce them. Religious leaders are not "authorities" on the subject of god and hell, etc., because god and hell cannot be studied and examined.

Statistics, of course, if properly obtained and honestly presented, are also authoritative. While statistics don't lie, they require intelligence to properly interpret them. For example, statistics show that every four seconds a woman gives birth to a baby, but that does not mean we have to find this woman and stop her before she overpopulates the universe. Logical thinking also depends upon the premise that there is such a thing as "knowledge" and "public facts" that can be ascertained with certainty or reasonable certainty, whether all people agree with that or not. "The evidence of the heavenly witnesses—the Father, the Word, and the Holy Ghost—would now be rejected in any court of Justice," said Gibbon.

Knowledge Is Real And Reliable

Textbooks on rational thinking say that both the content and the ultimate evaluation of arguments are comprised of assertions of "knowledge." Only people with knowledge *and access* to *knowledge* are capable of critical, logical thinking. Never argue with an ignorant or uneducated person! Any claim to knowledge implies at least three things: belief, truth and justification in the form of evidence. (Knowledge = justified, true belief.) *Thus, it is simply not true that all ideas and beliefs are equal for purposes of correct thinking; equality relates only to civil, political rights, not to the truth or correctness of one's thoughts and values.* By that standard, most beliefs do not qualify as knowledge, *and uneducated people cannot seriously participate in rational arguments (which is why politics is irrational).*

Facts are not established by majority vote. *Most Americans believe that, in a democracy, every person has a legal right to decide what is a fact and what is not a fact, which is, of course, simply ignorance.* "We must follow the argument wherever it leads," said Socrates, meaning that we are not free to disregard the results it produces because they are inconvenient. Flew explains that, "To say that someone *knows something* is to say more than that he claims to know it, or that he believes it most strongly. It is to say also both that it is true and that he is in position to know that it is true." Truth can always be proved logically.

Common Fallacies

Most errors in thinking are due to "fallacies," meaning some kind of mistake in reason. Here are some common (and very popular!) fallacies that cause problems every day:

The Fallacy of Unknowable Fact: When an argument contains premises based on incomplete or conjectural facts, it involves this fallacy. "According to James Ussher, a sixteenth-century Anglican archbishop, and Dr. John Lightfoot, seventeenth century chancellor of St. Catherine's College in Cambridge, Creation occurred exactly 5,985 years ago." Christian preachers are constantly guilty of that.

The Fallacy of Popularity, often in the form of statements by famous people masquerading as "authorities." For example, Shirley MacLaine's book "explaining" psychic phenomena.

The Fallacy of Unqualified Authority, such as Pope John Paul II explaining that "true academic freedom must include the right of the faithful not to be troubled by theories that they are not expert in judging." Popes are not educators.

The pointless argument is another type of reasoning:

"Either God exists or I am a fool:

God exists.

Therefore I am not a fool." It is theoretically possible that god exists and you are a fool anyway.

Proving the negative to deny its opposite: For example, failure to prove that there are trolls under bridges in Germany or fairies in the gardens of Ireland does not mean that they do not exist, but is only a lack of proof.

Verbal fallacies (i.e., misuse of words) For example:

"Death is a subject of utmost gravity.

Thus, death keeps us from falling off the earth."

The false analogy fallacy: For example:

"There are public schools that teach secular humanism.

Secular humanism is believed in, like a religion.

Thus, religion can also be taught in public schools."

The fallacy of appealing to popular prejudice:

"The theory of evolution will destroy religion.

Godless teachers and textbooks are used in our schools.

"Thus, godless teachers should not be hired."

Reductio ad absurdam (taking a valid argument to an absurd extreme to make it look false):

"Good scientists have open minds.

People who deny Church authority have closed minds.

Darwin had a closed mind about evolution.

Therefore, Darwin was not a good scientist."

Division or composition of a group: For example, confusing an individual with a group of which he or it is a part, or vice versa:

"American Indians are disappearing.

That man is an American Indian.

Therefore, that man is disappearing."

Ambiguity and false equivalents is confusing, or misusing, a word that has two different meanings, such as the word "law," which can mean either manmade laws or scientific laws, or laws of nature. For example:

"All laws have a lawmaker.

The laws of gravitation and motion are laws.

Thus gravitation and motion have a lawmaker (god)."

Here's another: "If marriage is bliss, and if ignorance is bliss, then marriage is ignorance." And another:

"Everything God made is perfect," shouted the preacher.

"What about me?" a hunchback asked.

"You are a perfect hunchback," said the preacher.

The argument from ignorance. For example: "I don't care what you say, drinking alcohol is not at all the same as smoking pot. Pot makes people immoral and drinking does not."

The straw man fallacy: In this common strategy, you invent another enemy that is more easily attacked:

"Mary argued against prayer in the public schools.

Atheist Russia suppressed prayer in schools.

Therefore, Mary is advocating communism."

Misleading statement: Religious people say that "It is an historical fact that Jesus was known by his apostles to have risen from the dead." That sentence is false because it really says is what the apostles *thought*—not what actually happened to Jesus.

Cause-and-effect fallacy: Frank Buchman, founder of the conservative "Moral Re-Armament" movement in the 1950s, said: "I thank heaven for a man like Adolf Hitler, who built a first line of defense against the Anti-Christ of Communism." Thus, evil is good if it hurts your enemies!

The authoritative fallacy. Stalin once said, "Gaiety is the most outstanding feature of the Soviet Union." Religionists often think: if the Pope said it, it must be right.

Implied similarity (guilt by association): Given that communists oppose racism, Martin Luther King is a communist because he is opposed to racism.

Logical Thinking Should Be Taught In American Schools

Descartes wrote: "The chief cause of human error is to be found in prejudices picked up in childhood," which suggests that logical thinking should be taught in junior and senior high school. Vos Savant wrote: "First, we should study math ... which is just logic with numbers ... Second, we should study logical processes with particular attention to the fallacies. Third, in college and beyond, we should study practical applications of the art of reasoning, especially where it has political and economic ramifications."

But Can't A Rational Argument Be Made For God?

No. For an example of such an argument, Dr. Brand Blanshard, a Yale philosophy professor, attended a meeting of intellectuals and Roman Catholic officials in July, 1972. The religionists argued that god has revealed himself through the Bible, meaning that it is "holy truth" that reaches man through three "channels:" (1) Scripture, (2) tradition and (3) the Roman Catholic Church, which could all be proved by "reason". *They solve the "reason" problem by defining god himself as "reason" as well as "love." That takes care of that!* Religionists use words in special ways to mean only what they want them to mean (like Humpty Dumpty). Blanshard pointed out other obvious thinking errors, to no avail: "But if … respect for reason is adhered to, I do not see how the Roman Catholic can retain his present belief in revelation. He is committed to the view that revealed truth cannot be inconsistent with itself, he said. Yet the Bible is full of inconsistencies and contradictions." *The Church fathers have simply decreed that the Bible, since it is by definition revealed truth, cannot have inconsistencies!* That is, if there are inconsistencies we are not reading it right, and if there are intellectual problems, that is because there are "mysteries" that only god can know. So there! The religionists do not win arguments like that; they simply refuse to give words their dictionary meaning, making themselves undefeatable. Blanshard concluded that "Christianity is so full of fraud, that any honest man should repudiate the whole shebang and espouse Atheism. Ingersoll wrote: "A fact never went into partnership with a miracle. Truth scorns the assistance of wonders. A fact will fit every other fact in the universe, and that is how you can tell whether it is or is not a fact. A lie will not fit anything except another lie."

Atheism Allows Us To Create A Rational Life

Dan Barker wrote: "There is joy in rationality, happiness in clarity of mind. Free thought is thrilling and fulfilling—absolutely essential to mental health and happiness." If there is no god, nobody can tell *you* what "the good life" is: *you* have to figure it out for yourself. Dr. Ellis said that a mentally healthy, rational life should be built around the following personal traits: "self-interest, self-direction, social interest, tolerance, acceptance of ambiguity, acceptance of reality, commitment, risk-taking, self-acceptance, rationality and scientific thinking." Who could be against those things? When people seriously lack those traits or when they have extreme opposing behaviors, "We often consider them to be at least somewhat emotionally disturbed," he said. "The good principles of living can be advanced by unbelief, skepticism and atheism, which are normal and healthy. Mentally healthy people largely assume responsibility for their own lives and work out their own problems … Religiosity and self-sufficiency are contradictory terms," he wrote. "Devout, deity-inspired religionists tend to sacrifice human love for godly love and are frequently deficient in social competence," he said. "Certainly serious religionists are intolerant, because it is the other side of their coin."

"Emotionally mature people accept the fact that we live in a world of probability and chance, where there are no, nor probably ever will be, complete certainties … If one of the requisites for emotional health is acceptance of ambiguity and uncertainty, then divinity-oriented religiosity is the unhealthiest state imaginable," Ellis wrote. He also said "Rational people are almost by definition happier than devout religionists." "Life is a tragedy for those who feel, and a comedy for those who think," wrote La Bruyere. Wouldn't you rather be smart?

Fundamentalists, of course, fear public education. "You can educate yourself right out of a relationship with God," said Tammy Faye Bakker (before she and her husband got caught embezzling church funds).

Each person has to create his/her own life, which is what atheism and agnosticism are all about: thinking honestly and consistently. *It is difficult for a rational person to "take charge of his own life" without giving up religion.* Sartre said: "Man is nothing else but that which he makes of himself. That is the first principle of existentialism." It is also the first principle of atheism in general. "The unexamined life is not worth living," said Socrates. Almost all rational counselors of neurotic people say that living a self-motivated life is an ethical good worth striving for. *A religious person cannot live a rational life in the contemporary sense of that word.*

Camus said "Do not wait for the last judgment. It happens every day." Nietzsche asked "What is … Christian morality? Chance robbed of its innocence; unhappiness polluted with the idea of "sin;" well-being represented as a danger, as a "temptation"; a physiological disorder produced by the canker worm of conscience." "Happy or not, life is the only treasure a man possesses; those who do not love life do not deserve it," said Casanova (who was experienced enough to know!) "Man is born to live, not to prepare for life," said Pasternak. Psychologists and other wise men tell us that the Good Life includes a sense of humor, which is a sign of mental balance and of good judgment.

Anatole France said it first: "Make love now, by night and by day, in winter and in summer … You are in the world for that and the rest of life is nothing but vanity, illusion, waste. There is only one science, love; only one riches, love; only one policy, love. To make love is all the law, and the prophets." Which is better, using your sexual organs naturally here on earth or sacrificing your life so you can get to heaven and listen to organ music continuously?

"Optimism is irreconcilable with Christianity," said Schopenhauer. John Updike, probably America's foremost "serious" novelist, when asked the question "After Christianity, what?" answered: "Sex, in its many permutations, is surely the glue, ambiance, and motive force of the new humanism." Christians are taught that sex—which makes the world go around—is a duty that should not be enjoyed for its own sake! Without healthy sex, our species will die out!

America belongs to atheists too—and we also mourn.

CHAPTER 8

POLITICAL FOOTBALL

"There is no more reason to believe that man is descended from an inferior animal than there is to believe that a stately mansion has descended from a small cottage .... Man is not a mammal ... . If we have to give up either religion or education, we should give up education ... . All the ills from which America suffers can be traced to the teaching of evolution."

—William Jennings Bryan

Bryan was the 1896 Democratic nominee for President. Here we are, a century later, and that's exactly what Tom DeLay, House Republican Whip, and Attorney General John Ashcroft say every day, and nobody is laughing! It was very popular then, and believed to be true by a majority of Americans then, and it is believed to be true by a majority of Americans now! Uneducated political leaders are laughable but unfunny, like, for example: the joke's on us! "The enemy isn't conservatism. The enemy isn't liberalism. The enemy is bullshit," said Lars-Erik Nelson.

What is Politics?

In Webster's dictionary it is defined, among other things, as: "the art or science concerned with winning and holding control over a government," or "political activities characterized by artful and often dishonest practices." Without politics, there would be fewer comedians. "I just watch the Government and report the facts," said Twain. "Everything is changing: people are now taking comedians seriously and the politicians as jokes," said Will Rogers. Groucho said "Politics is the art of looking for trouble, finding it everywhere, diagnosing it incorrectly, and applying the wrong remedies."

Congress consists of 535 members, most of whom, according to public comedians, are people who violate the law. "The American system of justice is not perfect," Leno explained. "Now and then an innocent person is sent to the legislature." The idea of Congress trying to impeach a President for letting a babe give him some minor sexual pleasure is absurd, considering the moral standards of the average Congressman. Some subversive statistician recently provided to the Internet the following data applicable to our Congress:

28 accused of spousal abuse

7 arrested for fraud

19 accused of writing bad checks

117 have bankrupted at least two businesses

3 have been arrested for assault

71 could not get a credit card due to bad credit

14 have been arrested on drug related charges

21 are current defendants in lawsuits

84 were stopped for drunk driving in 1998 alone

"It could probably be shown by facts and figures that there

is no distinctly native American criminal class except Congress," said Twain. "Congress consists of one third, more or less, scoundrels; two thirds, more or less, idiots; and three thirds, more or less, poltroons," said Mencken. It has been said that some Congressmen are so upset about how much the government pays farmers not to grow wheat, they want more money not to accept bribes. There is no evidence that any of them felt unqualified to impeach Clinton for some heavy (no pun intended) petting. *Newsweek* reported recently that 87 Congressman are currently having affairs. "That is why they have roll call every morning," said Leno.

Machiavelli focused on this obvious point: "Politics has no relation to morals," he said. During the impeachment trial, Jesse Jackson was Clinton's "spiritual adviser." He, too, fathered a child out of wedlock. "In fact," said Leno, "that's where Bill and Monica got that cigar." (According to historians, the following Presidents had extra-marital affairs while in office: Clinton, Harding, Jackson, Jefferson, L.B. Johnson, Kennedy, F.D. Roosevelt and Washington. Newt Gingrich, another of Bill Clinton's moralist attackers, subsequently withdrew from public life himself because of his non-marital sexual escapades, which he thought were secret.

The Republicans Are Clever And The Democrats Are Dummies

The Republicans have now played the religion card, and have trumped the slow-thinking Democrats. Now, the function of a Congressman has been expanded to include protecting religion (and god) from the Democrats, communists and intellectuals! The Republicans make a big point of opposing homosexuality (implying that it is something Democrats recommend). "If homosexuality were normal, God would have created Adam and Bruce," said Anita Bryant, a born-again Miss America.

Lyndon Johnson, in his early school-teacher days, was

asked by his local Texas school board about the shape of the earth. "I can teach it round or flat," he replied, which shows the flexibility of mind that made him a great Southern, rural politician. In the same vein, W has discovered that he gets more votes by saying he is sure the Bible is all true (making all our science teachers liars).

P. J. O'Rourke said: "God is a Republican and Santa Claus is a Democrat." That is the basic difference between the Republicans and the Democrats: the Republicans believe that mankind is basically bad and must be controlled, and the Democrats think mankind is basically okay and should be cut a lot of slack (which is why they are accused of lacking "values.") In regard to the 2000 election, Leno said: "If God had wanted us to vote, he would have given us candidates." "As far as the men who are running for president are concerned, they aren't even people I would date," said Nora Ephron.

John Ashcroft holds Pentecostal prayer meetings in his office every day, even though only some of his staff are Fundies. He also gives speeches at Bob Jones "University" (sic) and spent $8,000 of the public's money to cover up the (partially naked!) classic-style statues representing *Justice* and *Law* at the Department of Justice building. He told the Christian magazine *Charisma:* "It's said that we shouldn't legislate morality. Well, I think all we should legislate is morality!" Morality now means religion.

For the first time in its history, the Republican Party favors interfering in the personal lives of all citizens, like "Big Brother" in Orwell's book, *1984.* Barry Lynn, executive director of *Americans United for Separation of Church and State* (himself a Christian minister), said of Ashcroft: "The bigger worry is that he has a fundamental misunderstanding of the separation of church and state and of the legitimate role of religion in public life. Ashcroft has been quick to promote his specific theological beliefs in the form of legislative initiatives." According to him, Ashcroft attacked our judicial system at the Christian Coalition's 1998 convention like this: "A robed elite have taken the wall of separation designed to protect religion and they have made it a wall of religious oppression." *He is so uneducated that he thinks the Constitution was originally intended to protect religion!* The new unofficial Republican "enforcer," Tom DeLay, told 300 people at a Baptist Church in Texas that god is using him to promote a "Biblical worldview" in politics, and that he pursued Bill Clinton's impeachment because he held "the wrong worldview."

Our President, W, said publicly that "atheists should not be considered patriots, or even citizens. This is one nation under God, damn it!" He has also said "Now don't get me wrong, folks, the Muslims and Jews are gonna burn in Hell forever, along with everyone else who doesn't believe in Jesus." This is nothing new: "It is for the good of the state that man should be deluded by religion," said Marcus Terentius Varro (116-27 BC).

Thorstein Veblen, a leading early 20th century American economist, would agree with the Republicans' new strategy: "As a general rule the classes that are low in economic efficiency, or in intelligence, or both, are peculiarly devout ..., especially in those sections which are backward in education, in the stage of development of their industry, or in respect to their contact with the rest of the industrial community."

Prof. Bloom said "The paradoxical result of the liberation of reason is greater reliance on public opinion for guidance, which weakens independence. Unless there is some strong ground for opposing majority opinion, it inevitably prevails. This is the really dangerous form of the tyranny of the majority."

Barry Goldwater would roll over in his grave if he heard the Republican leaders of today. He wrote: "There is no more powerful ally one can claim in a debate than Jesus Christ, or God, or Allah, or whatever one calls this supreme being. But like any powerful weapon, the use of God's name on one's behalf should be used sparingly. The religious factions that are growing throughout our land are not using their religious clout with wisdom. They are trying to force government leaders into following their position 100 percent. If you disagree with these religious groups on a particular moral issue, they complain, they threaten you with a loss of money or votes or both. *I'm frankly sick and tired of the political preachers across this country telling me as a citizen that if I want to be a moral person, I must believe in "A, B C and "D."* Just who do they think they are? And from where do they presume to claim the right to dictate their moral beliefs to me? I am warning them today: I will fight them every step of the way if they try to dictate their moral convictions to all Americans in the name of "conservatism."

What the Democrats need now—desperately—is somebody like Goldwater! It may well be that Bill Bradley was unsuccessful in running for nomination because he refused to adopt the Fundies' platform: "The only way to be true to our American tradition is to maintain absolute governmental neutrality regarding religious beliefs and practices," he said. What chance did Bradley have?

Fundies Are The Enemies Of Americanism

Our present government has expressed great respect for Pat Robertson, who is one of those weird people who actually believes that he personally controlled the weather. He ran for the Presidential nomination only a few years ago on a platform that was boldly illegal: "We have enough votes to run this country … and when the people say, 'we've had enough,' we're going to take over!" If anybody can destroy American democracy, he can. "I believe that he [Jesus] is Lord of the government, and the church, and business and education, and hopefully, one day, Lord of the press. I see him involved in everything. And that's why I don't want to stay just in the church, as such. I want the church to move into the world." He once was quoted by *Time* magazine as saying that god had spoken to him, directed his actions or heeded his prayers to "steer away a hurricane." The article also said he had reported a conversation with "Satan," who said: "Jesus is playing you for a sucker, Robertson."

Clearly, Fundies and other conservatives are not only against Democrats, they are against our courts, which constitute a separate branch of our government. According to them, the public enemy is "judges who go against popular opinion." That, of course, is exactly why our Founding Fathers made the judiciary separate from the legislative and the executive branches: judges are supposed to be not responsive to public opinion, which changes from year to year. Armstrong said "Robertson founded Regent University to train students to "take over" when the Kingdom of God arrives."

Here is a clear statement by Gary Bauer (of the so-called Family Research Council), showing that the Fundies' politics is a form of mind control and indoctrination, as practiced in communist Russia: "We are engaged in a social, political and cultural war. There's a lot of talk in America about pluralism. But the bottom line is somebody's values will prevail. *And the winner gets the right* to *teach our children what* to *believe."* Stalin said the same thing. *In 2002, the Texas Republican Party adopted a document that pledges* to *"restore the original intent of the First Amendment ... and dispel the myth of the separation of Church and State."* In other words, religionists are simply liars who think the public cannot possibly know anything about American history.

C. W. Dalton, in *The Right Brain and Religion,* said "It is little wonder that these generally ignorant, seedy, morally shoddy types (televangelists) achieve amazing success. They are treated as sacrosanct by a government fearful of offending religion." According to *The Washington Post,* Robertson said "The feminist agenda is not about equal rights for women. It is a socialist, anti-family political movement that encourages women to leave their husbands, kill their children, practice witchcraft and become lesbians." Is he insane?

The only way a Congressman can be popular with all his constituents, even though he benefits only his important ones, is to lie. Vos Savant wrote: "Politicians use false argument more than anyone else ..." Also, she said "We humans tend to believe what we're told unless we take the trouble to find out otherwise, and few of us have the inclination, the time, or even the means to accomplish such an investigation. This is one of the most serious weaknesses inherent in a democracy that values "one man (or woman), one vote."

In American politics, the appearance of old-fashioned, simple virtue is what gets everybody elected, rather than a candidate's actual character. For example, in the case of these three actual, real-life historical examples, the voters' choices seem rather easy:

Candidate A: associated with crooked politicians and consults with astrologists, has had two wives, chainsmokes and drinks 8 to 10 martinis a day.

Candidate B: kicked out of office twice, sleeps until noon, used opium, and drinks a quart of whisky every evening.

Candidate C: a decorated war hero, a vegetarian, doesn't smoke, drinks an occasional beer and hasn't had any extramarital affairs.

In fact, Mr. A above describes Roosevelt, Mr. B describes Churchill and Mr. C describes Hitler. Unfortunately, prudish, narrow-minded people don't always get what they deserve. The Germans voted for an upright, moral and narrow-minded, harmless-looking guy with a Charlie Chaplin mustache who painted watercolors, and got Satan personified. The religious speeches of Robertson and Buchanan are every bit as mean and dangerous as Hitler's.

Dr. Bob Kaufman, a senior leader of the New York Society

for Ethical Culture, remarked that "each of the candidates wants to carry a bigger *Bible* than the other one, and they're all hitting each other with it. " Prof. Kurtz said "There's supposed to be no test for running for political office, but we do have a litmus test now. You have to express piety."

The Separation Of Church And State

So the big question in politics today is: who thought up this lie about separating church and state? Conservative Republicans are not only against Democrats; they are against our courts, which constitute a separate branch of our government. According to them, the public enemy is "judges who go against popular opinion." Buchanan talks a lot about impeaching judges who give politically unpopular opinions: "Who are beneficiaries of the Court's protection? Members of various minorities including criminals, atheists, homosexuals, flag burners, illegal immigrants (including terrorists), convicts, and pornographers." Real Republicans, it appears, think that atheists are criminals deserving of punishment!

The Fundies, now backed by the Republicans, are on a roll! For example, Robertson said: "There is no such thing as separation of church and state in the Constitution. It is a lie of the Left and we are not going to take it anymore." Also: "When any civil government steps outside the mandate authorized by God Almighty, then that government does not have any further claim over its citizens."

The beauty of this new "conservative" strategy is that criticism by learned, prominent citizens no longer matters! For example, Prof. Norman Dorsen said "Zealous groups threaten to infringe civil liberties when they seek government support to impose their own religious views on non-adherents. This has taken many forms, including attempts to introduce organized prayer in public school, to outlaw birth control and abortion and to use public tax revenues to finance religious schools."

Barry Lynn said "If you allow people with religious agendas to set government policy based on their religion, you change a country from the democracy we have to the kind of religiously run country you find in Iran."

America Has Never Been "A Christian Nation."

Under President Washington in 1797, America made a treaty with Tripoli, declaring that "the government of the United States is not, in any sense, founded on the Christian religion," which was approved by the Senate under President John Adams without controversy. Madison said: "What influence, in fact, have ecclesiastical establishments had on society? In some instances they have been seen to erect a spiritual tyranny upon the ruins of the civil authority; on many instances they have been seen upholding the thrones of political tyranny; in no instance have they been the guardians of the liberties of the people … A just government, instituted to secure and perpetuate it, needs them not." John Adams said "Nothing is more dreaded than the national government meddling with religion." Madison also said "Religious bondage shackles and debilitates the mind and unfits it for every noble enterprise."

According to Lynn R. Buzzard of the Christian Legal Society, "Not only were a good many of the revolutionary leaders more deist than Christian, the actual number of church members was rather small. Perhaps as few as five percent of the populace were church members in 1776."

Martin Cartners, in *Steve Allen on the Bible, Religion & Morality*, asked: "How many conservatives, who talk constantly about restoring America's Christian heritage, have you heard mention that Washington, John Adams, Franklin, Jefferson, and most of the other founding fathers, as well as Lincoln, were not Christians? It was Washington who insisted that no reference to God appear in the Constitution." The government of the United States is not in any sense founded on the Christian religion.

Jefferson said: "Shake off all the fears of servile prejudices, under which weak minds are servilely crouched. Fix reason firmly in her seat, and call on her tribunal for every fact, every opinion. *Question with boldness even the existence of a God, because, if there be one, he must more approve of the homage of reason than that of blind faith ...*"

Similarly, he wrote: "We should all then, like the Quakers, live without an order of priests, moralize for ourselves, follow the oracle of conscience, and say nothing about what no man can understand, nor therefore believe ... And the day will come, when the mystical generation of Jesus, by the Supreme Being as his Father, in the womb of a virgin, will be classed with the fable of the generation of Minerva in the brain of Jupiter."

At a dinner for Washington and Hamilton, Jefferson said "The way to see by Faith is to shut the Eye of Reason." Also, he said "Because religious belief or non-belief is such an important part of every person's life, freedom of religion affects every individual. State churches that use government power to support themselves and force their views on persons of other faiths undermine all our civil rights. Moreover, state support of the church tends to make the clergy unresponsive to the people and leads to corruption within religion. Erecting the 'wall of separation between church and state,' therefore, is absolutely essential in a free society." Madison said "An alliance or coalition between Government and religion cannot be too carefully guarded against ... Every new and successful example therefore of a PERFECT SEPARATION between ecclesiastical and civil matters is of importance that religions and government exist in greater purity without, rather than with the aid of government." *Are atheists the only people who know things like that?*

In his autobiography Jefferson wrote that "an amendment was proposed by inserting the words, "Jesus Christ, the holy author of our religion," which was rejected "by a great majority, in proof that they meant to comprehend, within the mantle of its protection, the Jew and Gentile, the Christian and the Mohammedan, the Hindoo *and the Infidel of every denomination."*

President John Adams once said "… this would be the best of all possible worlds, if there were no religion in it." Even Lincoln took religion with a grain of salt, remaining seated when his pastor asked all to rise who wanted to go to heaven and next (on seeing Lincoln still seated), asked all to rise who wanted to go to hell. In response to the pastor's next question, Lincoln quipped, "I plan to go to Congress."

The fundamental American law on the separation of church and state is clear and overwhelming. Henry Clay (a Southerner) said "All religions united with government are more or less inimical to liberty. All, separated from government, are compatible with liberty." Jimmy Carter said "I am not in favor of the government mandating a prayer in school because our country was founded on the fact that no particular religious faith would have ascendance over or preferential treatment over any other."

The Supreme Court said "We repeat and again reaffirm that neither a State nor a the Federal Government can constitutionally force a person 'to profess a belief or disbelief in any religion.' Neither can constitutionally pass laws or impose requirements which aid all religions as against non-believers, and neither can aid those religions based on a belief in the existence of God as against those religions founded on different beliefs." *(Murray v. Curlett.)*

Our President, W, should read the following complaint by one of the early presidents of Yale (a very religious man), who complained bitterly about our new Constitution as follows: "The nation has offended Providence. We formed our Constitution without any acknowledgment of God; without any recognition of His mercies to us, as a people, of His government, or even of His existence." This, of course, proves that prominent citizens during the founding of our country *were clearly aware that god was not a part of it.*

In *Lee v. Weisman* the Supreme court decided that the Constitution is violated "whenever government action creates an identification of the state with a religion, or with religion in general ... or when the effect of the governmental action is to endorse one religion over another, or to endorse religions in general." All Constitutional lawyers and civil litigators know that. Article VI, Section 3, of the Constitution provides another obstacle to religion: "... no religious test shall ever be required as a qualification to any office or public trust under the United States." (In communist Russia, of course, they solved historical facts by rewriting the history books, which is what the Fundies do every day.)

When the law tries to run people's lives without any democratic, public purpose, people break the law all the time. For example, a Connecticut law against contraceptives was estimated to be broken (joyously and eagerly, no doubt) every night by tens of thousands of law-abiding citizens before it was overturned for having *no secular purpose. In other words, it seems to be settled once and for all that the government has no power to enforce religious morals.* Justice Jackson (dealing with release of public school children for religious instruction) wrote: "The day that this country ceases to be free for irreligion, it will cease to be free for religion."

F. Lee Bailey said it all: "Can any of you seriously say the Bill of Rights could get through Congress today? *It wouldn't even get out of* committee. Martin Mayer, President of Christian Action Network, said "I do have a problem with separation of church and state. I don't think there's any thing wrong with the government having religious views and practices." Now imagine a prominent Democrat saying: "I'm not going to obey policemen any more until the law is changed to prohibit speeding tickets." He would be laughed out of office next time around.

Even some religionists are shocked by the stupid things Fundies say. Robert Coles, a prominent pediatrician, psychiatrist and essayist who is himself a religious believer, recently wrote a book called "The Secular Mind" in which he notes the tendency of our times for politicians to inject religion into our public life. Reynolds Price, a popular writer sympathetic to Coles, wrote the following comment is his book review: "The public voice of ethical and spiritual propaganda as it flows, for example, from the Christian right in America, poses a constant and urgent question. If these promoters are expressing the results of their particular sacred thoughts, then aren't many quite common kinds of sacred thinking genuinely dangerous to our freedom, our legacy of tolerance and sympathy and ultimately our sanity? *In fact, it is possible* to *argue cogently that sacred thought in the hands of politicians can have very little* to *offer a population as various as our own.* From papal Europe in the Middle Ages to David Koresh's commune, past examples of theocracy are hardly models for private or civic emulation."

Our Courts Settled These Issues Many Years Ago

The Christian Right would reimpose belief in god as a requirement to be heard in court. For example, in a 1809 case involving Connecticut law, the court said "There can be no doubt but that the law intended, that the fear of offending God should have its influence upon a witness to induce him to speak the truth. But no such influence can be expected from the man who disregards an oath." In 1820 a New York court ruled that a disbeliever in god and a future state of rewards and punishments could not be a witness in court because ... "in the development of facts, and the ascertainment of truth, no testimony is entitled to credit, unless delivered under the solemnity of an *oath.*"

Similarly, in 1846 New York adopted a constitution that provided ambiguously that no person shall be "incompetent" on account of his "opinions on matters of religious belief." The Ohio supreme court held in 1877 that "one who did not believe in God could not subscribe to the oath, and hence he could not be competent as a witness." Until recent years, the Arkansas constitution provided that "No person who denies the being of a God shall be competent to testify as a witness."

Even in the 19th century, the courts commonly allowed witnesses and jurors to be questioned as to their religious beliefs (or lack thereof). In the 1908 case of *Gambrell v. State*, a Mississippi court reversed a murder conviction on the ground of error in the exclusion of a defense offer of a witness to show that the deceased, whose dying declaration was the only positive proof as to who did the killing, was an "infidel" whose declaration could be impeached. In the case of *State v. Turner*, a 1908 South Carolina case involving an accused who testified in his own defense, it was held that he could be asked in cross examination whether or not he had made certain declarations regarding religion.

Even worse is the practice of applying such rules to defendants themselves, on the theory that they were also "witnesses," making any defense at all difficult if not impossible, depending upon the jurors. According to one court, the statutory requirement that a witness be "conscientiously scrupulous of taking an oath" meant that the witness had to believe in … the power of that Deity to accomplish punishment."

Even today, some states, including Iowa and Ohio, which constitutionally preclude any religious tests for determining the competency of witnesses, still permit questions as to religious belief for purposes of "impeaching," or casting doubt upon, truth or falsity of statements by a witness. Under those kinds of rules, many defendants were effectively convicted because they were non-believers! Belief was also required for jury qualification, under the same kind of rationale. As recently as 1924, a North Carolina court disqualified an atheist on the ground that, by denying the existence of god, he is presumed to be insensible to the obligations of an oath.

The Pledge Of Allegiance To God

Most people think something called the "Pledge of Allegiance" is a legal requirement for citizenship. They don't know that it has no law of any kind behind it, and is just a patriotic slogan, devised in the twentieth century by some obscure citizen with nothing else to do. When in June of 2002 a U.S. Court of Appeals held the words "under God" to be unconstitutional in a public school pledge of allegiance exercise, it was like a bombshell in Washington. What most people disliked was that it was not the court's decision that was so unusual, but that the plaintiff was an ATHEIST! (No mention was made of atheism as a logical or illogical belief, and the decision would have been the same if the plaintiff has not been an atheist.) Rush Limbaugh then said "This isn't going to stand! It's asinine! This is great! This is going to elect Republicans all over the country." This clever strategy, of course, has the drawback that it is not ethical. The result of that case should be discussed in civics class in all public schools, but the teachers and principals haven't the guts for it; they know their kids' parents are unreasonable, so why risk their jobs? The laughs keep coming: Fundies immediately hailed that event as "legal" proof that our government is *under god!"*

A similar false argument conservatives make to show the Constitution is based on Christianity is that our coins say "In God We Trust." In other words, a slogan put on our coins in 1954 (which does not constitute an amendment of the Constitution or any other law) now determines how the Constitution must be read! When Jesse Ventura, a prominent political libertarian, was asked recently which of our Constitutional rights are threatened most by current political trends, he said: "The separation of church and state. I think the founding fathers believed religion shouldn't interact directly with government. There is no right religion, and no one can prove that there is." On the question of a mandatory pledge of allegiance, Jesse said "... it isn't the government's job to mandate patriotism. To me, mandating a pledge of allegiance to a government is something Saddam Hussein would do ..." Urgent question: Are professional wrestlers smarter than Yale graduates?

Grass-roots Republicans Now Push "Creationism"

A key plank in the Republicans' new "populist strategy" is support for Bible study in the public schools, to be known as "Creationism." In order to get elected, or to stay in power, grass-roots activists have mounted an expensive, no-holds-barred national campaign designed to require Bible teaching in public school science classes. Instead of calling it Bible study they have coined the word "Creationism" to make it sound "scientific." All that is required is to provide "an alternate explanation" of geologic layers of rock and the bones of animals and humans. (Somewhere in the Bible there is a mention of rocks and rivers!) The American scientific community is virtually 100% opposed to them, but "hearings" are now being held in many states to decide whether Bible studies can qualify as "science." In order to be "fair," these hearings have now involved local politicians as well as the two parties involved. Guess how a politician would break a tie vote!

When asked for his opinion about the Creationism litigation in Kansas recently, Prof. Gould said (according to *The New York Times*): "... the citizens of Kansas would be profoundly embarrassed by the stupidity of the ruling and that they would vote that school board out of office the next year. The Kansas School Board's decision is absurd on the face of it." (The decision was later reversed.)

In "The Man With No Endorphins," James Gorman

wrote: "The creation/evolution conflict is good fun—as conflicts go—certainly better than, say, a *thermonuclear conflict*, or the Super Bowl ... I can show that preachers and chimpanzees are quite a lot alike ... All I'm saying is that Pat Robertson is a chimpanzee's relative, and acts like one, as do we all. The apes are my relatives, I'm proud to have them, and I don't intend to vote for anybody who isn't related to them, or is ashamed to admit it ... I have one question for each presidential candidate: are you kin to the apes or not? Once we know, we'll know how to vote." Based on his public statements about religion, W could not pass that test.

The Republicans are keeping a low profile on this because it is obviously bad for education, although a real winner for politics. Tom DeLay said that the problem was teaching children "that they are nothing but glorified apes who are evolutionized out of some primordial soup of mud." That should get a "10" on any comedian's laugh-meter. Nixon once said: "What are schools for if not indoctrination against communism?" Pat Buchanan takes the same fascistic position. DeLay also claimed that "Christianity offers the only viable, reasonable, definitive answer to the questions of "Where did I come from? Why am I here? Where am I going? Does life have any meaningful purpose?" Since DeLay is an uneducated man (a former termite exterminator), it may be unfair to criticize him for not knowing anything about American history.

Science buff Robert Heinlein said "When any government, or any church for that matter, undertakes to say to its subjects, "This you may not read, this you may not see, this you are "forbidden to know, the end result is tyranny and oppression ... Mighty little force is needed to control a man whose mind has been hoodwinked; contrariwise, no amount of force can control a free man, a man whose mind is free. No, not the rack, not fission bombs, not anything—you cannot conquer a free man; the most you can do is kill him."

This is no idle threat: books are still being banned in America *right now* by Christian zealots, as described in "100 Banned Books," by Nicholas J. Karolides, Margaret Bald and Dawn D. Sova. In that book are all the facts you need about the recent banning or attempted banning of some of the best books ever written, including, for example: *Black Boy*, by Richard Wright; *The Grapes of Wrath*, by John Steinbeck; *1984*, by George Orwell; *Uncle Tom's Cabin*, by Harriet Beecher Stowe; *The Ugly American*, by Lederer and Burdick; *An American Tragedy*, by Theodore Dreiser; *The Bluest Eye.."* by Toni Morrison; *The Group*, by Mary McCarthy; *Leaves of Grass ..."* by Walt Whitman; *Of Mice and Men,"* by John Steinbeck; and *To Kill a Mockingbird*, by Harper Lee.

Since most people don't even know how to think freely, they won't even notice it when free-thinking and free writing are banned, as Attorney General Ashcroft wants to do *in the name of morality*.

RECOMMENDED READING

Among many others, the author has consulted the following books and Internet websites related to the subjects of religion, science, rational thinking and atheism which a reader might find rewarding. This is not, however, a complete, scholarly bibliography (because this is not a scholarly book, but a book designed as entertainment). Some additional references have been incorporated into the text of each chapter. As mentioned in the Foreword, this book summarizes the thoughts of others and invents nothing new. None of the quotations or jokes included in this book are those of the author.

Adler, Mortimer J. *How to Think About the Great Ideas.* Open Court, 2000.

Altizer, J. and Mortimer J. Adler. *Radical Theology and the Death of God.* Bobbs-Merril, 1966.

Altizer, Thomas J. *The Gospel of Christian Atheism.* Westminster, 1966.

Armstrong, Karen. *A History of God.* Knopff, 1994.

Beirce, Ambrose. *The Devil's Dictionary.* Oxford, 1999.

Blackburn, Simon. *Think.* Oxford U., 1999.

Bloom, Allan. *The Closing of the American Mind.* Simon and Schuster, 1987.

Byrd, Eldon A. *How Things Work.* Parker, 1973.

Campbell, Joseph. *Myths to Live By.* Viking Press, 1972.

Carey, Stephen J. *A Beginner's Guide to Scientific Method.* Wadsworth, 1998.

Chase, Stuart. *Guides to Straight Thinking.* Harper and Row, 1956.

Dick, Stephen J. *Many Worlds.* Tempeleton Foundation, 2000.

Dictionary of the History of Ideas. Ed. Phillip P. Wiener. Scribners, 1973.

Ellis, Albert, Ph.D. *The Case Against Religion.* American Atheist.

Flew, Anthony. *How to Think Straight.* Prometheus, 1998.

Flew, Anthony. *A Dictionary of Philoshopy.* Grammercy, 1979.

Fox, Robin Lane. *The Unauthorized Version.* Knopf, 1991.

Gould, Stephen J. *Rocks of Ages—Science and Religion in the Fullness of Life.* Ballantine, 1999.

Grinnel, Frederick. *The Scientific Attitude.* Guilford, 1992.

Haught, James A. *2000 Years of Disbelief: Famous People with the Courage to Doubt.* Prometheus, 1996.

Kahane, Howard and Nanacy Cavender. *Logic and Contemporary Rhetoric.* Wadsworth, 1998.

Krueger, Douglas. *What is Atheism?* Prometheus, 1998.

Kurtz, Paul. *Living Without Religion.* Prometheus, 1994.

Logical Positivism. Ed. A.J. Ayer. The Free Press, 1959.

Martin, Steve. *Pure Drivel.* Hyperion, 2002.

McGuinness, Brian. *Wittgenstein: A Life.* U. of California, 1998.

McGinn, Colin. *The Mysterious Flame.* Basic, 1999.

O'Shea, Stephen. *The Perfect Heresy.* Walker, 2000.

Phares, E. Jerry. *Introduction to Personality.* Scott Foresman, 1988.

Pinker, Stephen. *How the Mind Works.* W.W. Norton, 1997.

Seldes, George. *The Great Thoughts.* Ballantine, 1985.

Shils, Edward A. *Tradition.* U. of Chicago, 1981.

Smith, George H. *Atheism—The Case Against God.* Prometheus, 1989.

Smith, Warren Allen. *Celebrities in Hell.* Barricade, 2002.

Soccio, Douglas J. and Vincent E. Barry. *Practical Logic*. Harcourt, Brace Jovanovich, 1992.

Taves, Anne. *Fits, Trances and Visions*. Princeton, 1999.

Tieger, Paul D. and Barbara Barron-Tieger. *Do What You Are*. Little Brown, 2001.

Vos Savant, Marilyn. *Logical Thinking*. St. Martins Griffin, 1998.

Wills, Gary. *Papal Sins*. Doubleday, 2000.

Wright, Robert. *The Moral Animal*. Random House, 1994.

Internet:

www.Xs4all.nl~jcdverha/scijokes

www.netfunny.com/rhf/jokes

www.physlink.com/fm/jokes.cfm

www.workjoke.com/projoke37

www.ahajokes.com/science